## World University Library

The World University Library is an international series
of books, each of which has been specially commissioned.
The authors are leading scientists and scholars from all over
the world who, in an age of increasing specialisation, see the
need for a broad, up-to-date presentation of their subject.
The aim is to provide authoritative introductory books for
university students which will be of interest also to the general
reader. The series is published in Britain, France, Germany,
Holland, Italy, Spain, Sweden and the United States.

*Frontispiece*. The visual region of the brain – the *area striata*.
Here we see a small part of the mechanism of the brain highly
magnified. These cell bodies with their connections handle
information from the eyes, to give us knowledge of the world.

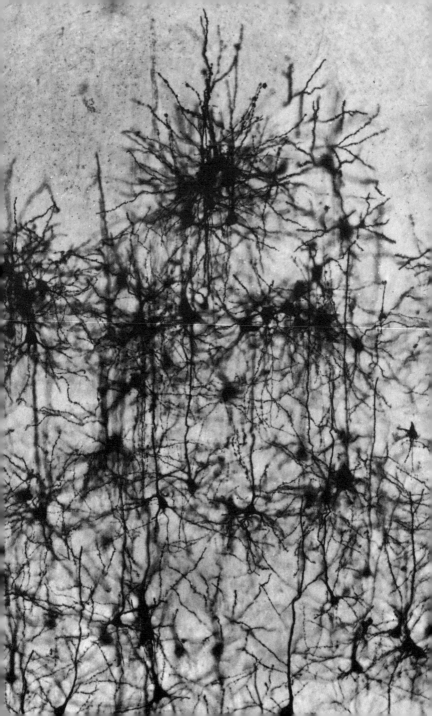

R. L. Gregory

# Eye and Brain

**the psychology of seeing**

**World University Library**

**McGraw-Hill Book Company**
**New York  Toronto**

First published March 1966
Second impression June 1966
Third impression January 1967
Fourth impression March 1969
Fifth impression September 1970
Second edition 1973
Reprinted 1974
Reprinted 1976


*Library of Congress Cataloging in Publication Data*
Gregory, Richard Langton.
**Eye and brain.**

(World university library)
Bibliography: p.
1. Vision.   I. Title.
BF241.G7   1973   152.1'4   72-3792
ISBN 0-07-024661-0 clothbound
ISBN 0-07-024660-2 paperbound

Photoset by BAS Printers Limited, Wallop, Hampshire
Manufactured by LIBREX, Milan, Italy

# Contents

# 1 Seeing

We are so familiar with seeing, that it takes a leap of imagination to realise that there are problems to be solved. But consider it. We are given tiny distorted upside-down images in the eyes, and we see separate solid objects in surrounding space. From the patterns of stimulation on the retinas we perceive the world of objects, and this is nothing short of a miracle.

The eye is often described as like a camera, but it is the quite uncamera-like features of perception which are most interesting. How is information from the eyes coded into neural terms, into the language of the brain, and reconstituted into experience of surrounding objects? The task of eye and brain is quite different from either a photographic or a television camera converting objects merely into images. There is a temptation, which must be avoided, to say that the eyes produce pictures in the brain. A picture in the brain suggests the need of some kind of internal eye to see it – but this would need a further eye to see *its* picture . . . and so on in an endless regress of eyes and pictures. This is absurd. What the eyes do is to feed the brain with information coded into neural activity – chains of electrical impulses – which by their code and the patterns of brain activity, represent objects. We may take an analogy from written language: the letters and words on this page have certain meanings, to those who know the language. They affect the reader's brain appropriately, but they are not pictures. When we look at something, the pattern of neural activity represents the object and to the brain *is* the object. No internal picture is involved.

Gestalt writers did tend to say that there are pictures inside the brain. They thought of perception in terms of modifications of electrical fields of the brain, these fields copying the form of perceived objects. This doctrine, known as isomorphism, has had unfortunate effects on thinking about perception. Ever since, there has been a tendency to postulate properties to these hypothetical brain fields such that visual distortions, and other phenomena, are 'explained.' But it is all too easy to postulate things having just the right properties. There is no independent evidence for such brain fields, and no independent way of discovering their properties. If there is no evidence for them, and no way of discovering their properties, then they are highly suspect. Useful explanations relate observables.

The Gestalt psychologists did however point to several important phenomena. They also saw very clearly that there is a problem in how the mosaic of retinal stimulation gives rise to perception of objects. They particularly stressed the tendency for the perceptual system to group things into simple units. This is seen in an array of dots (figure 1·1). Here the dots are in fact equally spaced, but there is a tendency to see, to 'organise,' the columns and rows as though there are separate objects. This is worth pondering, for in this example we have the essential problem of perception. We can see in ourselves the groping towards organising the sensory data into objects. If the brain were not continually on the look-out for objects, the cartoonist would have a hard time. But, in fact, all he has to do is present a few lines to the eye and we see a face, complete with an expression. The few lines are all that is required for the eye – the brain does the rest: seeking objects and finding them whenever possible. Sometimes we see objects which are not there: faces-in-the-fire, or the Man in the Moon.

Figure 1·2 is a joke figure which brings out the point clearly. Just a set of meaningless lines? No – it is a washer-woman with her bucket! Now look again: the lines are subtly different, almost solid – they are objects.

The seeing of objects involves many sources of information beyond those meeting the eye when we look at an object. It generally involves knowledge of the object derived from previous experience, and this experience is not limited to vision but may include the other senses; touch, taste, smell, hearing and perhaps also temperature or pain. Objects are far more than patterns of stimulation: objects have pasts and futures; when we know its past or can guess its future, an object transcends experience and becomes an embodiment of knowledge and expectation without which life of even the simplest kind is impossible.

1·1 This array of equally spaced dots is seen as continually changing patterns of rows and squares. We see something of the active organising power of the visual system while looking at this figure.

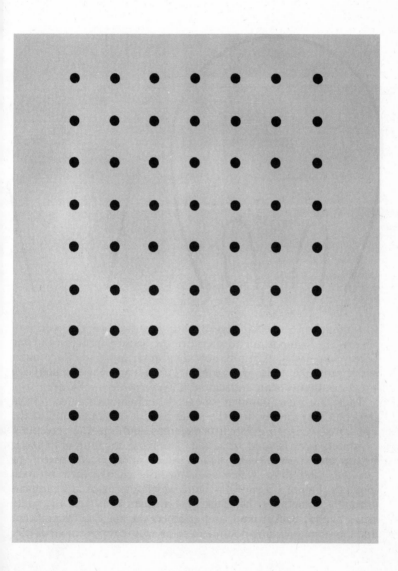

1·2 A joke figure – what is it? When you see it as an object, not merely meaningless lines, it will suddenly appear almost solid – an *object*, not a *pattern*.

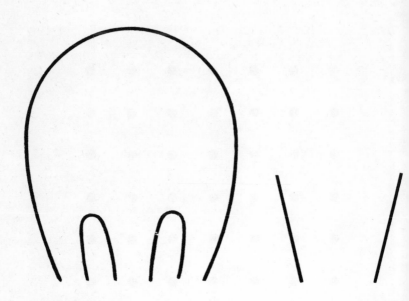

Although we are concerned with how we see the world of objects, it is important to consider the sensory processes giving perception – what they are, how they work and when they fail to work properly. It is by coming to understand these underlying processes that we can understand how we perceive objects.

There are many familiar so-called 'ambiguous figures,' which illustrate very clearly how the same pattern of stimulation at the eye can give rise to different perceptions, and how the perception of objects goes beyond sensation. The most common ambiguous figures are of two kinds: figures which alternate as 'object' or 'ground,' and those which spontaneously change their position in depth. Figure 1·3 shows a figure which alternates in figure and ground – sometimes the black part appears as a face, the white being neutral background, and at others the black is insignificant and the white surround dominates and seems to represent an object.

1·3 This figure alternates spontaneously, so that sometimes it is seen as a pair 11
of faces, sometimes as a white urn bounded by meaningless black areas –
the faces. The perceptual 'decision' of what is figure (or object) and what
ground, is similar to the engineer's distinction between 'signal' and 'noise'
It is basic to any system which handles information.

The well-known Necker cube (figure 1·4) shows a figure alternating
in depth. Sometimes the face marked with the 'o' lies in front,
sometimes at the back – it jumps suddenly from the one position
to the other. Perception is not determined simply by the stimulus
patterns; rather it is a dynamic searching for the best interpretation
of the available data. The data is sensory information, and also
knowledge of the other characteristics of objects. Just how far
experience affects perception, how far we have to learn to see, is a
difficult question to answer; it is one which will concern us in this
book. But it seems clear that perception involves going beyond the
immediately given evidence of the senses: this evidence is assessed
on many grounds and generally we make the best bet, and see
things more or less correctly. But the senses do not give us a picture
of the world directly; rather they provide evidence for checking
hypotheses about what lies before us. Indeed, we may say that a

1·4 This figure alternates in depth: the face of the cube marked by the small circle sometimes appearing as the *front*, sometimes as the *back* face.
We can think of these ways of seeing the figure as perceptual 'hypotheses'.
The visual system entertains alternative hypotheses, and never settles for one solution. This process goes on throughout normal perception, but generally there is a unique solution.

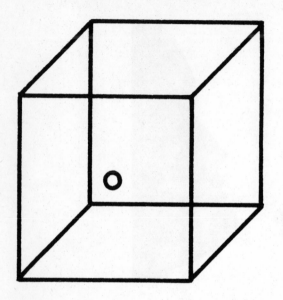

perceived object *is* a hypothesis, suggested and tested by sensory data. The Necker cube is a pattern which contains no clue as to which of two alternative hypotheses is correct: the perceptual system entertains first one then the other hypothesis, and never comes to a conclusion, for there is no best answer. Sometimes the eye and brain come to wrong conclusions, and then we suffer hallucinations or illusions. When a perceptual hypothesis – a perception – is wrong we are misled, as we are misled in science when we see the world distorted by a false theory. Perceiving and thinking are not independent: 'I see what you mean' is not a puerile pun, but indicates a connection which is very real.

# 2 Light

To see, we need light. This may seem too obvious to mention but it has not always been so obvious – Plato thought of vision as being due not to light entering, but rather to particles shot out of the eyes, spraying surrounding objects. It is difficult to imagine now why Plato did not try to settle the matter with a few simple experiments. Although to philosophers the problem of how we see has always been a favourite topic of speculation and theory, it is only in the last hundred years that it has formed the object of systematic experiments; which is odd, because all scientific observations depend upon the human senses – most particularly upon sight.

For the last three hundred years there have been two rival theories of the nature of light. Isaac Newton (1642–1737) argued that light must be a train of particles, while Christopher Huygens (1629–95) argued that it must be pulses – which he thought of as small elastic spheres in contact with each other – travelling through an all-pervading medium, the *aether*. Any disturbance, he suggested, would be carried in all directions through the packed spheres as a wave, and this wave is light.

The controversy over the nature of light is one of the most exciting and interesting in the history of science. A crucial question in the early stages of the discussion was whether light travelled at a finite speed, or whether it arrived instantaneously. This was answered in a quite unexpected way by a Danish astronomer, Roemer (1644–1710). He was engaged in recording eclipses of the four bright satellites orbiting round Jupiter, and found that the times he observed were not regular, but depended upon the distance of Jupiter from the earth.

He came to the conclusion, in 1675, that this was due to the time light took to reach him from the satellites of Jupiter, the time increasing when the distance increased, because of the finite velocity of light. In fact, the distance of Jupiter varies by about 300,000,000 km. (twice the distance of the sun), and the greatest time-difference he observed was 16 minutes 36 seconds earlier or later than the calculated time of the eclipses of the satellites.

2·1 Christopher Huygens (1629–95) by an unknown artist.
He argued that light travels as waves, through an aether.

From his somewhat faulty estimate of the distance of the sun he calculated the speed of light as 309,000 km. per second. With our modern knowledge of the diameter of the earth's orbit, we correct this to a velocity of about 300,000 km. per second, or $3 \times 10^{10}$ cm/sec. The speed of light has since been measured very accurately over short distances on earth, and it is now regarded as one of the basic constants of the Universe.

Because of the finite velocity of light, and the delay in nervous messages reaching the brain, we always see the past. Our perception of the sun is over eight minutes late; all we know of the furthest object visible to the unaided eye (the Andromeda nebula) is so out of date that we see it as it was a million years before men appeared on Earth.

The value of $3 \times 10^{10}$ cm/sec for the speed of light strictly holds only for a perfect vacuum. When light travels through glass or water, or any other transparent substance, it is slowed down to a velocity which depends upon the refractive index (roughly the density) of the medium through which it is travelling. This slowing down of light is extremely important, for it is this which causes prisms to bend light, and lenses to form images. The principle of refraction (the bending of light by changes of refractive index) was first understood by Snell, a Professor of Mathematics at Leyden, in 1621. Snell died at thirty-five, leaving his results unpublished. Descartes published the Law of Refraction eleven years later. The Law of Refraction (The 'Sine Law') is:

> When light passes from a medium A into a medium B the sine of the angle of incidence bears to the sine of the angle of refraction a constant ratio.

We can see what happens with a simple diagram (figure 2·3): if AB is a ray passing from a dense medium into a vacuum (or air) the ray will emerge into the air at some angle i along BD.

The Law states that $\dfrac{\sin i}{\sin r}$ is a constant. The constant is the refractive index known as $v$.

Newton thought of his corpuscles of light as being attracted to the surface of the denser medium, while Huygens thought that the bending was due to the light travelling more slowly in the denser medium. It was many years before the French physicist Foucault showed by direct measurement that light does indeed travel more slowly in a denser medium. It seemed for a time that Newton's corpuscle theory of light was entirely wrong – that light is purely a series of waves radiating through a medium, the *aether* – but at the beginning of the present century it was dramatically shown that the wave theory does not explain all the phenomena of light. It now seems that light is both corpuscles and waves.

Light consists of packets of energy – *quanta* – these combining the characteristics of corpuscles and waves. Light of short wavelength has more waves in each bundle than light of longer wavelength. This is expressed by saying that the energy of a single quantum is a function of frequency, such that $E = hv$ where $E$ is the energy in ergs, $h$ is a small constant (Planck's constant) and $v$ is the frequency of the radiation.

When light is bent by a prism, each frequency is deviated through a slightly different angle, so that the emergent beam comes out of the prism as a fan of light, giving all the spectral colours. Newton discovered that white light is a compound of all the spectral colours, by splitting a beam of sunlight into a spectrum in this way and then finding that he could re-combine the colours back into white light by passing the spectrum through a second similar prism, held the other way up.

Newton named seven colours for his spectrum – red, orange, yellow, green, blue, indigo, violet. One does not really see indigo as a separate colour, and orange is a bit doubtful. What happened is that Newton liked the number 7 and added the names orange and indigo to make the magic number!

We know now, though Newton did not, that each spectral colour, or hue, is light of a different frequency. We also know that all so-called electromagnetic radiation is essentially the same. The physical difference between radio waves, infra-red, light, ultraviolet

2·2 Sir Isaac Newton (1642–1727) by Charles Jervas. On the whole, Newton held that light consists of particles, but he was aware of many of the difficulties, anticipating the modern theory that light has the dual properties of particles and waves. He devised the first experiments to show that white light is a mixture of the spectral colours, and paved the way to an understanding of colour vision by elucidating the physical characteristics of light.

2·3 Light is bent (refracted) by a dense transparent medium. The ratio of the sines of the angles of the rays entering and leaving the dense medium are constant for a given refractive index of the medium. This is the basis of image formation by lenses. (The angle of deviation of light is also a function of the wavelength of light, so that a beam is split into the spectral colours by a prism.) The lettering is explained in the text.

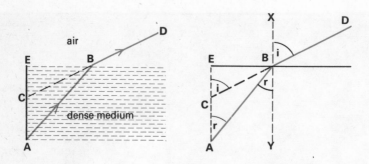

and X-rays is their frequency. Only a very narrow band of these frequencies, less than an octave in width, stimulates the eye to give vision and colour. The diagram (figure 2·5) shows how this narrow window fits into the physical picture. Looked at in this way, we are almost blind.

If we know the speed of light and its frequency, it is a simple matter to calculate its wavelength, but in fact its frequency is difficult to measure directly. It is easier to measure the wavelength of light than its frequency; though this is not so for the low frequency radio waves. The wavelength of light is measured by splitting it up not with a prism, but with a grating of finely ruled lines, which also produces the colours of the spectrum. (This can be seen by holding an L.P. record at an oblique angle to a source of light, when the reflection will be made up of brilliant colours.) Given the spacing of the lines of a grating, which are specially ruled, and the angle producing light of a given colour, wavelength may be determined very accurately. It turns out that the blue light has a wavelength of about $\frac{1}{70,000}$ of an inch while the wavelength of red light is about $\frac{1}{40,000}$ of an inch. The wavelength of light is important for it sets the limit to the resolution of optical instruments.

2·4 A freehand sketch by Newton of one of his experiments on colour.
He first split light into a spectrum (with the large prism), then allowed
light of a single colour to pass through a hole in a screen to a second prism.
This did not produce more colours. He also found that a second prism
placed in the spectrum would recombine the colours into white.
Thus white light is made up of all the colours of the spectrum.

We cannot with the unaided eye see individual quanta of light,
but the receptors in the retina are so sensitive that they can be
stimulated by a single quantum, though several (five to eight) are
required to give the experience of a flash of light. The individual
receptors of the retina are as sensitive as it is possible for any light
detector to be, since a quantum is the smallest amount of radiant
energy which can exist. It is rather sad that the transparent media
of the eye do not quite match this development to absolute perfection. Only about ten per cent of the light reaching the eye gets
to the receptors, the rest being lost by absorption and scattering
within the eye before the retina is reached. In spite of this loss, it
would be possible under ideal conditions to see a single candle
placed seventeen miles away.

The quantal nature of light has an important implication for vision, which has inspired some particularly elegant experiments bridging the physics of light and its detection by the eye and brain. The first experiment on the effect of light being packaged into quanta was undertaken by three physiologists, Hecht, Shlaer, and Pirenne, in 1942. Their paper is now a classic. Realising that the eye must be almost if not quite as sensitive as theoretically possible, they devised a most ingenious experiment for discovering how many quanta actually accepted by the receptors are required to see a flash of light. The argument is based on a statistical function known as the *Poisson distribution*. This gives the expected distribution of hits on a target. The idea is that part at least of the moment-to-moment variation in the effective sensitivity of the eye is not due to anything in the eye or the nervous system, but to the variation in moment-to-moment energy of weak light sources. Imagine a desultory rain of bullets: they will not arrive at a constant rate, but will fluctuate; similarly there is fluctuation in the number of light quanta that arrive. A given flash may contain a small or large number of quanta, and is more likely to be detected if there happen to be more than the average number of quanta in the flash. For bright lights, this effect is unimportant, but since the eye is sensitive to but a few quanta, the fluctuation is important near the minimal energy required for detection.

The quantal nature of light is also important in considering the ability of the eye to detect fine detail. One of the reasons why it is possible to read only the largest newspaper headlines by moonlight, is that there are insufficient quanta falling on the retina to build up a complete image within the time-span required by the eye to integrate energy – about a tenth of a second. In fact this is not by any means the whole story; but the purely physical factor of the quantal nature of light contributes to a well known visual phenomenon – loss of acuity in dim light – which until recently has been treated purely as though it were a property of the eye. Indeed, it is often quite difficult to establish whether a visual effect should be regarded as belonging to psychology, physiology or physics. They get pretty well mixed up.

2·5 Light is but a narrow region of the total electromagnetic spectrum, which includes radio waves, infra red, ultra violet and X-rays. The physical difference is purely the wavelength of the radiation, but the effects are very different. Within the octave to which the eye is sensitive, different wavelengths give different colours. Beyond light these are very different properties when radiation interacts with matter.

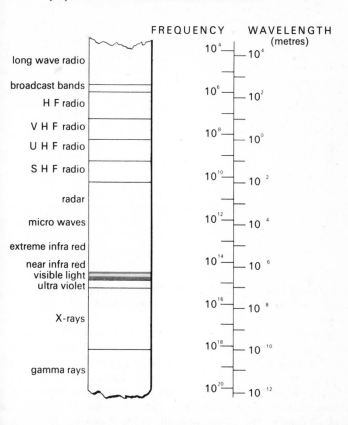

How are images produced? The simplest way an image can be formed is by a pin hole. Figure 2·6 shows how this comes about. A ray from a part of the object (x) can only reach one part of the screen (y) – the part lying along the straight line passing through the pin-hole. Each part of the object illuminates a corresponding part of the screen, so an upside-down picture of the object is formed on the screen. The pin-hole image will be rather dim, for

2·6 Forming an image with a pinhole. A ray from a given region of the source reaches only a single region of the screen – the ray passing through the hole. Thus an (inverted) image is built up from the rays lying in the path of the hole. The image is free from distortion, but is dim and not very sharp. A very small hole introduces blurring through diffraction effects, due to the wave nature of light.

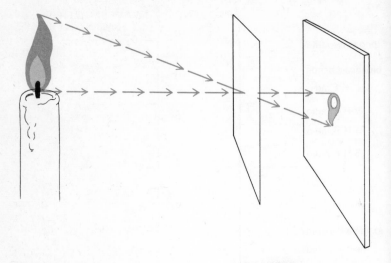

the hole must be small if the image is to be sharp. (Though if it is *too* small it will be blurred because the wave structure of the light is upset).

A lens is really a pair of prisms (figure 2·7). It directs a lot of light from each point of the object to a corresponding point on the screen, thus giving a bright image. Unlike pin-holes, lenses only work well when they are suitable, and adjusted correctly. The lens of the eye can be unsuitable to the eye in which it finds itself, and it can be adjusted wrongly. The lens may focus the image in front of or behind the retina, instead of on it, giving 'short' or 'long' sight. The lens may not be truly spherical in its surface, giving distortion and, in some directions, blurring of the image. The cornea may be irregular, or pitted (perhaps due to abrasion from metal filings in industry, or grit from riding a motor cycle without protective goggles). These optical defects can be corrected by adding artificial lenses–spectacles. Spectacles correct for errors in accommodation by changing the power of the lens of the eye;

2·7 A lens can be thought of as a pair of converging prisms, forming an image from a bundle of rays. The image is far brighter than from a pinhole, but it is generally distorted in some degree, and the depth of focus is limited. [This figure should not be taken too literally – image-forming lenses have curved surfaces.]

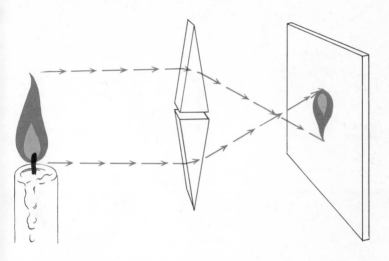

they correct for astigmatism by adding a non-spherical component. Ordinary spectacles cannot correct for damage to the surface of the cornea but the newer *corneal lenses*, fitted to the eye itself, serve to give a fresh surface to the cornea.

Spectacles lengthen our effective lives. With their aid we can see to read and to perform skilled tasks into old age: before their invention scholars and craftsmen were made helpless by lack of sight, though they still had the power of their minds.

3·1 Various primitive eyes. All of the ones here have the same basic plan: a lens forming an image on a mosaic of light-sensitive receptors.

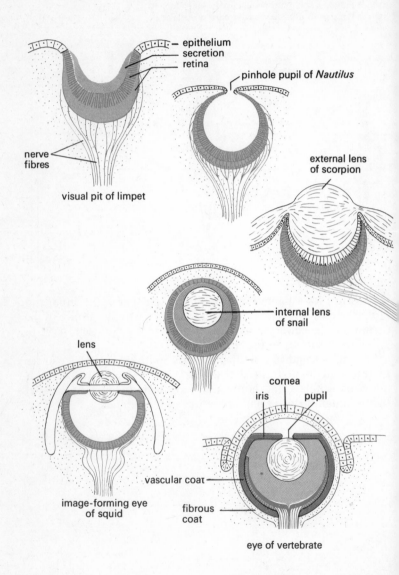

# 3 In the beginning . . .

Almost every living thing is sensitive to light. Plants accept the energy of light, some moving to follow the sun almost as though flowers were eyes to see it. Animals make use of light, shadows, and images to avoid danger and to seek their prey.

The first simple eyes responded only to light, and changing intensity of light. Perception of form and colour waited upon more complicated eyes capable of forming images, and brains sufficiently elaborate to interpret the neural signals from optical images on the retinas.

The later image-forming eyes developed from light-sensitive spots on the surface of simpler animals. How this occurred is largely mysterious, but we know some of the characters in the story. Some can be seen as fossils; some are inferred from comparative studies of living species; others appear fleetingly during the development of embryo eyes.

The problem of how eyes have developed has presented a major challenge to the Darwinian theory of evolution by Natural Selection. We can make many entirely useless experimental models when designing a new instrument, but this was impossible for Natural Selection, for each step must confer some advantage upon its owner, to be selected and transmitted through the generations. But what use is a half-made lens? What use is a lens giving an image, if there is no nervous system to interpret the information? How could a visual nervous system come about before there was an eye to give it information? In evolution there can be no master plan, no looking ahead to form structures which, though useless now, will come to have importance when other structures are sufficiently developed. And yet the human eye and brain have come about through slow painful trial and error.

Response to light is found even in one-celled animals. In higher forms, we find specially adapted cells to serve as receptors sensitive to light. These cells may be scattered over the skin (as in the earth worm) or they may be arranged in groups, most often lining a depression or pit, which is the beginning of a true image-forming eye.

It seems likely that photoreceptors became recessed in pits because there they lay protected from the surrounding glare which reduced their ability to detect moving shadows, heralding the approach of danger. Millions of years later, but for the same reason, early Greek astronomers dug deep holes in the ground, from which they could observe stars in the daytime.

The primitive eye pits were open to the danger of becoming blocked by foreign particles lodging within them, shutting out the light. A transparent protective membrane developed over the eye pits, serving to protect them. When, by chance mutations, this membrane became thicker in its centre, it became a crude lens. The first lenses served merely to increase intensity, but later they came to form useful images. An ancient pit type of eye is still to be seen in the limpet. One living creature, *Nautilus*, has an eye still more primitive – there is no lens, but a pin hole to form the image. The inside of the eye of *Nautilus* is washed by the sea in which it lives, while eyes with lenses are filled with specially manufactured fluids to replace the sea. Human tears are a re-creation of the primordial ocean, which bathed the first eyes (figure 3·1).

3·2 The fossil eye of a species of trilobite. This is the earliest kind
of eye preserved as a fossil. The facets are the corneal lenses,
essentially the same as a modern insect eye. Some trilobites
could see all round, but none above.

27

We are concerned in this book with human eyes, and how we see
the world. Our eyes are typical vertebrate eyes, and are not among
the most complex or highly developed, though the human brain is
the most elaborate of all brains. Complicated eyes often go with
simple brains – we find eyes of incredible complexity in pre-
vertebrates serving tiny brains. The compound eyes of arthropods
(including insects) consist not of a single lens with a retina of many
thousands or millions of receptors, but rather of many lenses with
but a single receptor element for each lens. The earliest known
fossil eye belongs to the Trilobites – which lived over 500,000,000
years ago – the earliest preserved fossils being found in Cambrian
rocks. In many species of trilobite, the eyes were highly developed.
The external structure of these most ancient eyes may be seen
perfectly preserved (figure 3·2). We can see nothing now of the
internal structure, only the outer form is tantalisingly with us now.
They were compound eyes, rather like those of a modern insect:
some had over a thousand facets.

Figure 3·3 shows an insect eye. Behind each lens facet ('corneal
lens') lies a second lens ('lens cylinder') through which light passes
to the light-sensitive element, this usually consisting of seven cells
grouped in a minute flowerlike cluster. Each complete unit of a
compound eye is known as an 'ommatidium.' It used to be thought
that each ommatidium is a separate eye – so that insects must see
thousands of worlds – but how this came to be believed is strange,
for there is no separate retina in each ommatidium, and but a
single nerve fibre from each little group of receptors. How then
could each one signal a complete image? The fact is that each
ommatidium signals the presence of light from a direction immediately in front of it, and the combined signals represent
effectively a single image.

Insect eyes have a particularly remarkable mechanism to give
dark or light adaptation. The ommatidia are isolated from each
other by black cones of pigment: with reduced light (or in response
to signals from the brain) the pigment migrates back towards the
receptors so that light can then pass through the side of each

ommatidium to neighbouring receptors. This increases the sensitivity of the eye, but at a cost to its acuity – a trade balance found also in vertebrate eyes, though for somewhat different reasons.

The lens cylinder of the compound eye does not function by virtue of the shape of its optical surfaces, as in a normal lens, so much as by change of its refractive index, which is greater near the centre than at its edge. Light is funnelled through it, in a way quite different from a normal lens. Compound eyes are principally detectors of movement, and can be incredibly efficient, as we know from watching a dragon fly catching its prey on the wing.

Among the most curious eyes in the whole of nature is that of a creature the size of a pin's head – a little known copepod – *Copilia*. She (the males are dull by comparison) has a pair of image-forming eyes, which function neither like vertebrate nor like compound eyes, but something like a television camera. Each eye contains two lenses, and the photoreceptor system is similar to the insect eye, but in *Copilia* there is an enormous distance between the corneal lens and the lens cylinder. Most of the eye lies deep within the body of the animal, which is extraordinarily transparent. She is shown in figure 3·4. The secret of this eye is to be found by looking at the living animal. Exner, in 1891, reported that the receptor (and attached lens cylinder) make a 'continuous lively motion.' They oscillate across the mid line of the animal, and evidently scan across the focal plane of the front corneal lens. It seems that the pattern of dark and light of the image is not given simultaneously by many receptors, as in other eyes, but in a time/series down the optic nerve, as in the single channel of a television camera. It is possible that many small compound eyes (e.g. *Daphnia*?) also go in for scanning to improve the resolution and channel capacity of their few elements. Is *Copilia*'s eye ancestral to the compound eye? Is scanning generally abandoned, because a single neural link could not transmit sufficient information? Is it a simplification of the compound eye found in the earliest fossils? Or is it perhaps an aberrant experiment, unrelated to the main streams of evolutionary

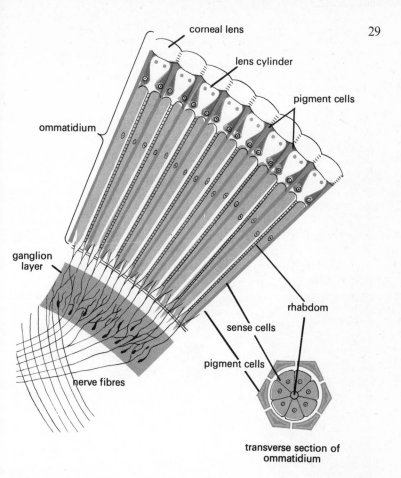

corneal lens

lens cylinder

pigment cells

ommatidium

ganglion layer

rhabdom

sense cells

pigment cells

nerve fibres

transverse section of
ommatidium

development? Whatever her status, *Copilia* deserves more recognition than she has received.

The scanning movement of the lens cylinder and the attached photoreceptor is shown by the successive frames of a cine film in figure 3·5. The receptors move precisely toward, then away from each other – never independently. The speed of the scan varies from about five per second to about one scan every two seconds.

One would give a lot to know why it exists, and whether it is the remaining example of a very early kind of eye. If *Copilia* is an evolutionary failure she deserves a prize for originality.

3·4 A living female specimen of a microscopic copepod, *Copilia quadrata*.
Each eye has two lenses: a large anterior lens and a second smaller
lens deep in the body, with an attached photoreceptor and single optic
nerve fibre to the central brain. The second lens and photoreceptor are
in continual movement, across the image plane of the first lens.
This seems to be a scanning eye: a mechanical television camera.

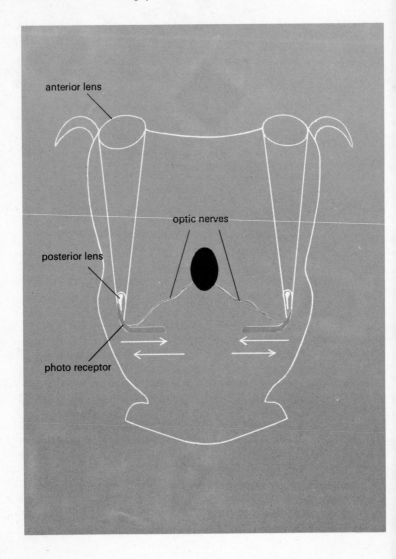

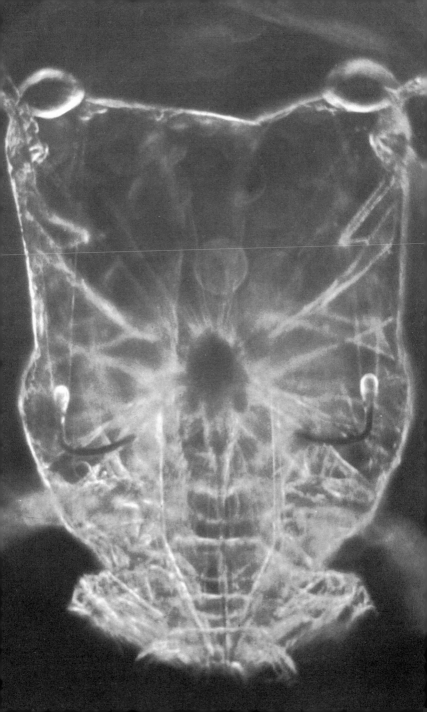

3·5 The posterior lens of *Copilia*, and attached photoreceptor (in red) during a single scan. The rate can be as high as 5 scans per second.

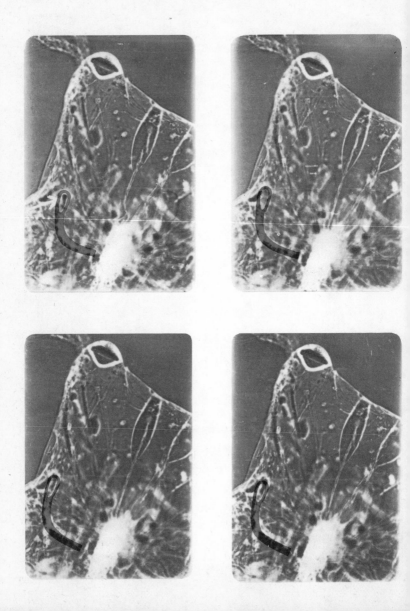

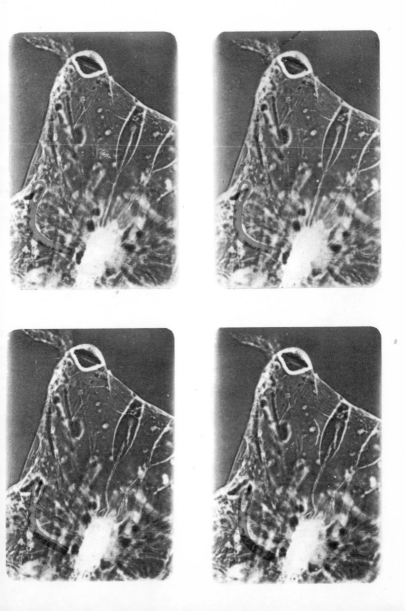

4·1 The human eye. The most important optical instrument. Here lies the focusing lens, giving a minute inverted image to an incredibly dense mosaic of light-sensitive receptors, which convert the patterns of light energy into the language the brain can read – chains of electrical impulses.

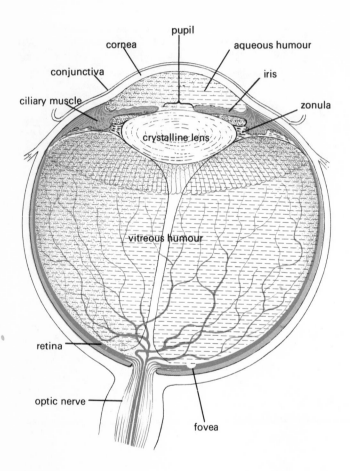

# 4 The eye

Each part of the eye is an extremely specialised structure (figure 4·1). The perfection of the eye as an optical instrument is a token of the importance of vision in the struggle for survival. Not only are the parts of the eye beautifully contrived, but even the tissues are specialised. The cornea is special in having no blood supply: blood vessels are avoided by obtaining nutriment from the aqueous humour. Because of this, the cornea is virtually isolated from the rest of the body. This is fortunate for it makes possible transplants from other individuals in cases of corneal opacity, since antibodies do not reach and destroy it, as happens to other alien tissues.

This system of a crucial structure being isolated from the blood stream is not unique to the cornea. The same is true of the lens, and in either case blood vessels would ruin their optical properties. It is also true of a structure in the inner ear, though here the significance is entirely different. In the cochlea where vibrations are converted into neural activity, there is a remarkable structure known as the *organ of Corti*, which consists of rows of very fine hairs joined to nerve cells that are stimulated by the vibration of the hairs. The organ of Corti has no blood supply, but receives its nutriment from the fluid filling the cochlea. If these very sensitive cells were not isolated from the pulse, we would be deafened. The extreme sensitivity of the ear is only possible because the crucial parts are isolated from the blood stream, and the same is true of the eye though for a different reason.

The aqueous humour is continually secreted and absorbed, so that it is renewed about once every four hours. 'Spots before the eyes' can be due to floating impurities casting shadows on the retina which may be seen as hovering in space.

Each eyeball is equipped with six extrinsic muscles, which hold it in position in its orbit, and rotate it to follow moving objects or direct the gaze to chosen objects. The eyes work together, so that normally they are directed to the same object, converging for near objects. Besides the extrinsic eye muscles, there are also muscles within the eyeball. The iris is an annular muscle, forming the pupil through which light passes to the lens lying immediately behind.

This muscle contracts to reduce the aperture of the lens in bright light, and also when the eyes converge to view near objects. Another muscle controls the focusing of the lens. We may look in more detail at the mechanism and function of the *lens* and the *iris*. Both have their surprises.

*The crystalline lens*. It is often thought that the lens serves to bend the incoming rays of light to form the image. This is rather far from the truth in the case of the human eye, though it is true for fishes. The region where light is bent most in the human eye to form the image is not the lens, but the front surface of the cornea. The reason for this is that the power of a lens to bend light depends on the difference between the refractive index of the surrounding medium and the lens material. The refractive index of the surrounding medium – air – is low, while that of the aqueous humour immediately behind the cornea is nearly as high as that of the lens. In the case of fish, the cornea is immersed in water, and so light is hardly bent at all when it enters the eye. Fish have a very dense rigid lens, which is spherical and moves backwards and forwards within the eye ball to accommodate to distant and near objects. Although the lens is rather unimportant for forming the image in the human eye, it is important for accommodation. This is done not by changing the position of the lens (as in a fish, or a camera) but by changing its shape. The radius of curvature of the lens is reduced for near vision, the lens becoming more powerful and so adding more to the primary bending accomplished by the cornea. The lens is built up of thin layers, like an onion, and is suspended by a membrane, the *zonula*, which holds it under tension. Accommodation works in a most curious manner. For near vision tension is released on the zonula, allowing the lens to spring to a more convex form, the tension being released by contraction of the ciliary muscle. It becomes more convex for near vision, by the muscle tightening and not relaxing, which is a surprising system.

The embryological and later developments of the lens are of

particular interest, and have dire consequences in middle life. The lens is built up from its centre, cells being added all through life, though growth gradually slows down. The centre is thus the oldest part, and there the cells become more and more separated from the blood system giving oxygen and nutrient, so that they die. When they die they harden, so that the lens becomes too stiff to change its shape for accommodation to different distances. As Gordon Walls puts it, in his great book *The Vertebrate Eye*:

> The lens is thus unique among the organs of the body in that its development never ceases, while its senescence commences even before birth.

We see this all too clearly in figure 4·2 which shows how accommodation falls off with age, as the starved cells inside the lens die, and we see through their corpses.

It is possible to see the changes in shape of someone else's lens as he accommodates to different distances. This requires no apparatus beyond a small source of light, such as a flashlight. If the light is held in a suitable position, it can of course be seen reflected from the eye, but there is not just one reflection – there are three. The light is reflected not only from the cornea, but also from the front and the back surfaces of the lens. As the lens changes its shape, these images change in size. The front surface gives a large and rather dim image which is the right way up, while the back surface gives a small bright image which is upside down. The principle can be demonstrated with an ordinary spoon. Reflected from the back convex surface you will see large right-way-up images, but the inside concave surface gives upside-down small images. The size of the images will be different for a large (table) spoon and a small (tea) spoon, corresponding to the curvatures of the lens of the eye for distant and near vision. (These images seen in the eye are known as Purkinje images, and are very useful for studying accommodation experimentally.)

*The iris.* This is pigmented, and is found in a wide range of colours. Hence the 'colour of a person's eyes' – which is a matter of some

4·2 (*Top*) Loss of accommodation of the lens of the eye with ageing. The lens gradually becomes rigid and cannot change its form. Bifocal spectacles serve to give effective change of focus when accommodation is lost.

4·3 (*Bottom*) Eye **a** cannot see into eye **b**. One's own eye always gets in the way, preventing light reaching the only part of the retina which could form an image.

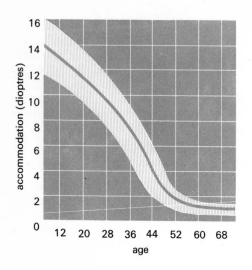

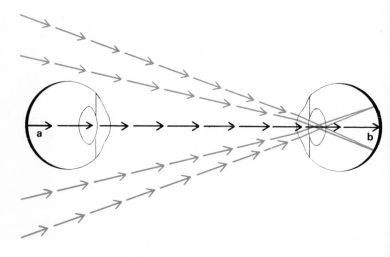

4·4 Making the iris oscillate with a beam of light. When the iris opens a little, more light reaches the retina, which then signals the retina to close. But when it closes less light reaches the retina, which signals the iris to open. Thus it oscillates. From the frequency and amplitude of oscillation the iris control system can be described in terms of servo-theory.

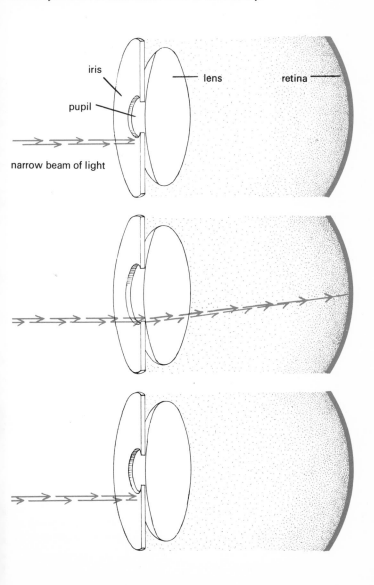

4·5 How eyes would look if we could see into them. This photograph is taken with an ophthalmoscope. It shows the yellow spot over the fovea, the retinal blood vessels through which we see the world, and the blind region where the vessels and nerves leave the eyeball.

interest to poets, geneticists and lovers, but less so to those concerned with the function of the eye. It matters not what colour the iris is but it must be reasonably opaque so that it is an effective aperture stop for the lens. Eyes where pigment is missing (albinism) are defective in strong light.

It is sometimes thought that the changes in pupil size are important in allowing the eye to work efficiently over a wide range of light intensities. This could hardly be its primary function however, for its area only changes over a ratio of about 16:1, while the eye works efficiently over a range of brightness of about 100,000:1. It seems that the pupil contracts to limit the rays of light to the central and optically best part of the lens except when the full aperture is needed for maximum sensitivity. It also closes for near vision, and this increases the depth of field for near objects.

To an engineer, any system which corrects for an external change (in this case light intensity) suggests a 'servo-mechanism.' These are very familiar in the form of the thermostats in central heating, which switch on the heat automatically when the temperature drops below some pre-set value, and then switch it off again when the temperature rises. (The earliest example of a man-made servo-mechanism is the windmill, which aims into the wind and follows its changing direction by means of the fantail sail, which rotates the top of the mill through gearing. A more elaborate example is the automatic pilot which keeps a plane on correct course and height by sensing errors and sending correcting signals to the control surfaces of the machine.)

To go back to the thermostat sensing temperature changes in a central heating system: imagine that the difference between the setting of the lower temperature for switching on the heat is very close to the upper temperature for switching it off. No sooner is it switched on than temperature will rise enough to switch it off again, and so the heating system will be switched on and off rapidly until something breaks. Now by noting how frequently it is switched on and off, and noting also the amplitude of the temperature variation, an engineer could deduce a great deal about the system. With this

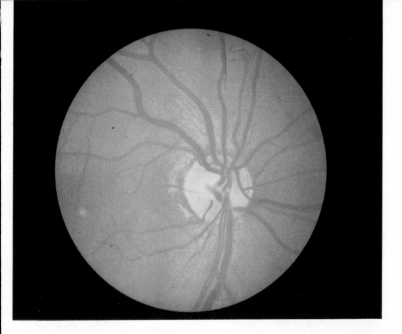

in mind, some subtle experiments have been performed on just how the iris servo-control system works.

The iris can be made to go into violent oscillation, by directing a narrow beam of light into the eye, so that it passes by the edge of the iris (figure 4·4). Now when the iris closes a little, the beam is partly cut off, and so the retina gets less light. But this gives the iris a signal to open. As soon as it opens the retina gets more light – and then the iris starts to close, until it gets another signal to open. Thus it oscillates in and out. By measuring the frequency and amplitude of oscillation of the iris a good deal can be learned about the neural servo-system controlling it.

*The pupil.* This is not, of course, a structure. It is the hole formed by the iris through which light passes to the lens and on to the retina as an image. Although the human pupil is circular, there is a great variety of shapes, the circular form being rather unusual. For some unknown reason, the eyes of nocturnal animals have slit-shaped pupils, most evident in the cat.

The pupil looks black, and we cannot see through it into another person's eye. This requires some explanation, for the retina is not

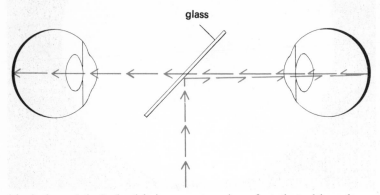

4·6 The principle of the ophthalmoscope, invented by Helmholtz. Light reaches the observed eye by reflection from a half-silvered mirror, through which the observer sees the inside of the eye. (In practice he may look above an illuminating ray directed into the eye with a small prism, which avoids the losses of the half-silvered mirror.)

black, but pink. Indeed it is a most curious fact that although we see out of our pupil, we cannot see into someone else's! The reason is that the lens in the other person's eye focuses light from any given position on to a certain region of the retina, so the observing eye always gets in the way of the light which would shine onto the part of the retina he should be seeing (figure 4·3). Helmholtz devised a simple device (the ophthalmoscope) for seeing into another person's eye, the trick being to direct a beam of light along the path the observer is looking (figure 4·6). With this device the pupil no longer looks black, and the detailed structure of the living retina may be seen, the blood vessels on its surface appearing as a great red tree of many branches.

## Eye movements

Each eye is moved by six muscles (figure 4·7). The remarkable arrangement of the *superior oblique* can be seen in the illustration. The tendon passes through a 'pulley' in the skull, in front of the suspension of the eye ball. The eyes are in continuous movement, and they move in various ways. When the eyes are moved around, searching for an object, they move quite differently from the way they move when a moving object is being followed with the eyes.

The eyeball is maintained in position in 43
the orbit by six muscles, which move it to direct the gaze to any position
and give convergence of the two eyes for depth perception. They are under
continuous tension and form a delicately balanced system, which when upset
can give illusions of movement.

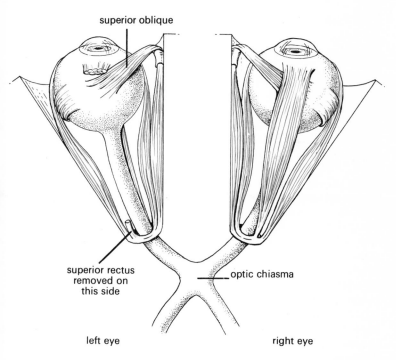

superior oblique

superior rectus
removed on
this side

optic chiasma

left eye                          right eye

When searching, they move in a series of small rapid jerks, but
when following they move smoothly. The jerks are known as
*saccades* (after an old French word meaning 'the flick of a sail').
Apart from these two main types of movement, there is also a
continuous small high-frequency tremor.

Eye movements can be recorded in various ways: they can be
filmed with a cine camera, detected by small voltage changes
around the eyes, or most accurately by attaching a mirror to a
contact lens placed on the cornea, when a beam of light may be
reflected off the mirror and photographed on continuously-moving
film.

It turns out that the saccadic movements of the eyes are essential to vision. It is possible to fix the image on the retina so that wherever the eye moves, the images move with it, and so remain fixed on the retina. When the image is optically stabilised (figure 4·8) vision fades after a few seconds, and so it seems that part of the function of eye movements is to sweep the image over the *receptors* so that they do not adapt and so cease to signal to the brain the presence of the image in the eye. But there is a curious problem: when we look at a sheet of white paper, the edges of the image of the paper will move around on the retina, and so stimulation will be renewed, but consider now the centre of the image. Here the small movements of the eyes can have no effect, for a region of given brightness is substituted for another region of exactly the same brightness, and so no change in stimulation takes place with the eye movements. Yet the middle of the paper does not fade away. This suggests that borders and outlines are very important in perception. Signals from large regions of constant brightness are not very important – for the visual system fills in between contours, reducing demands for channel capacity.

Blinking is often assumed to be a reflex, initiated by the cornea becoming dry. But for normal blinking this is not so; though blinking can be initiated by irritation of the cornea, or by sudden changes in illumination. Normal blinking occurs with no external stimulus: it is mediated by signals from the brain. The frequency of blinking increases under stress, and with expectation of a difficult task. It falls below average during periods of concentrated mental activity. Blink rate can even be used as an index of attention and concentration on a task. Whenever we blink we are blind, but we are not aware of it.

## The retina

The name retina is from an early word meaning 'net' or 'cobweb tunic,' from the appearance of its blood vessels.

The retina is a thin sheet of interconnected nerve cells, including the light-sensitive rod and cone cells which convert light into electrical pulses – the language of the nervous system. It was not always obvious that the retina is the first stage of visual sensation. The Greeks thought of the retina as providing nutrient to the vitreous. The source of sensation was supposed by Galen, and by much later writers, to be the crystalline lens. The Arabs of the middle ages – who were the keepers of classical knowledge – thought of the retina as conducting the vital spirit, the 'pneuma'.

It was the astronomer Kepler who, in 1604, first realised the true function of the retina – that it is the screen on which an image from the lens is formed. This hypothesis was tested experimentally by Scheiner, in 1625. He cut away the outer coating (the *sclera* and the *choriod*) from the back of an ox's eye, leaving the retina revealed as a semi-transparent film. Scheiner saw a small upside-down image on the retina of the ox's eye.

The discovery of the photoreceptors had to wait upon the development of the microscope and its systematic use. It was not until about 1835 that they were first described, and then none too accurately, by Treviranus. It seems that his observation was biased by what he expected to see, for he reported that the photoreceptors face the light. Strangely, they do not: in mammals and in nearly all vertebrates – though not in cephalopods – the receptors are placed at the back of the retina, behind the blood vessels. This means that light has to go through the web of blood vessels, and the fine network of nerve fibres – including three layers of cell bodies and a host of supporting cells – before it reaches the receptors. Optically, the retina is inside out, like a camera film put in the wrong way round (figure 4·9). Given the original 'mistake' however, (which seems to result from the necessary embryological development of the retina from the surface of the brain) the situation is largely saved by the nerve fibres from the periphery of the retina skirting around and avoiding the crucial central region giving best vision.

The retina has been described as 'an outgrowth of the brain.' It

4·8 A simple way of optically stabilising the retinal image. The object (a small photographic transparency), is carried on the eye on a contact lens, and moves exactly with it. After a few seconds the eye becomes blind to the stabilised image, some parts fading before others. This method was devised by R. Pritchard.

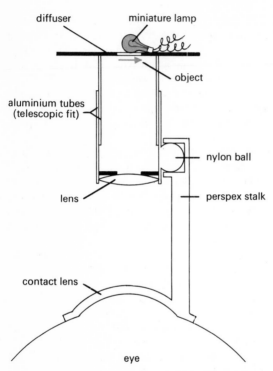

is a specialised part of the surface of the brain which has budded out and become sensitive to light, while it retains typical brain cells lying between the receptors and the optic nerve (but situated in the front layers of the retina) which greatly modify the electrical activity from the receptors themselves. Some of the data processing for perception takes place in the eye which is thus an integral part of the brain.

There are two kinds of light-receptor cells – the *rods* and the *cones* – named after their appearance as viewed with a microscope. In the peripheral regions of the retina they are clearly distinguish-

4·9 The retina. Light travels through the layers of blood vessels, nerve fibres and supporting cells to the sensitive receptors ('rods' and 'cones'). These lie at the back of the retina, which is thus functionally inside-out. The optic nerve is not, in vertebrate eyes, joined directly to the receptors, but is connected via three layers of cells, which form part of the brain externalised in the eyeball.

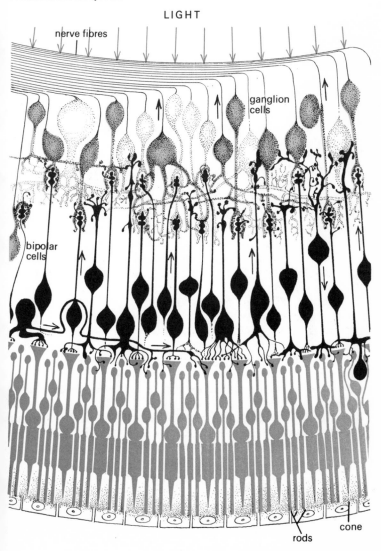

LIGHT

nerve fibres

ganglion cells

bipolar cells

rods

cone

able, but in the central region – the *fovea* – the receptors are packed exceedingly close together, and look like the rods.

The cones function in daylight conditions, and give colour vision. The rods function under low illumination, and give vision only of shades of grey. Daylight vision, using the cones of the retina, is referred to as *photopic* while the grey world given by the rods in dim light is called *scotopic*.

It might be asked how we know that the cones, and only the cones, mediate colour vision. It is deduced partly from studies of various animal eyes, by relating retinal structure to their ability to discriminate colours as determined by behaviour experiments; and also from the finding that in the human retina there are very few cones near the edge of the retina, where there is no colour vision. It is interesting that although the central foveal region, packed tightly with functional cones, gives the best visual detail and colour, it is less sensitive than the more primitive rod regions of the retina. (Astronomers 'look off' the fovea when they wish to detect very faint stars so that the image falls on a region of the retina rich in rods).

It might be said that, moving from the centre of the human retina to its periphery, we travel back in evolutionary time; from the most highly organised structure, to a primitive eye which does little more than detect movements of shadows. The very edge of the human retina does not even give a sensation when stimulated by movement: it merely initiates a reflex to direct the eyes to the source of movement, so that we can see it with our developed foveal eye.

The size of the receptors and their density become important when we consider the ability of the eye to distinguish fine detail. We shall quote directly from Polyak's great book *The Retina*:

> The central territory where the cones are almost uniformly thick measures approximately 100 $\mu$ (microns, or millionths of a metre) across, corresponding to 20', or one-third of a degree of arc. It contains approximately fifty cones in a line. This area seems to be not exactly circular but elliptical, with the long axis horizontal, and may contain altogether

2,000 cones. . . . the size of each of the 2,000 receptor-conductor units measures, on the average, 24″ of arc. The size of the units even in this territory varies, however, the central most measuring scarcely more than 20″ of arc or even less. Of these – the most reduced cones, and therefore the smallest functional receptor units – there are only a few, perhaps not more than one or two dozen. The size of the units given includes the intervening insulating sheaths separating the adjoining cones from one another.

It is worth trying to imagine the size of the receptors. The smallest, one micron, is only about two wavelengths of red light in size. One could not ask for much better than that. Even so, the visual acuity of the hawk is four times better than man.

The number of cones is about the same as the population of Greater New York. If the whole population of the United States of America were made to stand on a postage stamp, they would represent the rods on a single retina. As for the cells of the brain – if people were scaled down to their size, we could hold the population of the earth in our cupped hands; but there would not be enough people to make one brain.

The photopigments of the retina are bleached by bright light; it is this bleaching which – by some entirely mysterious process – stimulates the nerves, and it takes some time for the photochemical to return to normal. The retinal chemical cycle involved is now understood, primarily through the work of Dr George Wald. While a region of photopigment is bleached, this region of the retina is less sensitive than the surrounding regions, and this gives rise to *after-images*. When the eye has been adapted to a bright light (e.g. a lamp bulb viewed with the eye held steady, or better a photographic flash) a dark shape, of the same form as the adapting light, is seen hovering in space. It is dark when seen against a lighted surface, such as a wall, but for the first few seconds after stimulation by the adapting light, it will look bright when viewed in darkness. This is called a positive after-image, and represents continuing firing of the retina and optic nerve after the stimulation. When dark it is called a negative after-image, and represents the relatively reduced sensitivity of the stimulated part of the retina due partly to bleaching of the photopigment.

## Two eyes

Many of the organs of the body are duplicated, but the eyes, and the ears, are unusual in working in close co-operation: for they share and compare information, so that together they perform feats impossible for the single eye or ear.

The images in the eyes lie on the curved surfaces of the retinas, but it is not misleading to call them two-dimensional. A remarkable thing about the visual system is its ability to synthesise the two somewhat different images into a single perception of solid objects lying in three-dimensional space.

In man the eyes face forwards, and share the same field of view; but this is rare among vertebrates, for generally the eyes are at the sides of the head and aim outwards in opposed directions. The gradual change from sideways to frontal looking eyes came about as precise judgment of distance became important, when mammals developed front limbs capable of holding and handling objects, and catching the branches of trees. For animals who live in forests and travel by leaping from branch to branch, rapid and precise judgment of distance of nearby objects is essential; and the use of two eyes, co-operating to give stereo vision, is highly developed. Animals such as the cat have frontal eyes which function together, but the density of the receptors is nearly constant over the retina. There is no fovea unless precise depth perception is really important, as in birds and in the tree-living apes, when we find developed foveas and precise control of eye movements. Stereo vision for movement is also provided by the paired compound eyes of insects, and is highly developed in insects such as the dragon fly which catches its prey at high speeds on the wing. The compound eyes are fixed in the head, and the mechanism of their stereo vision is simpler than in apes and man where foveas are brought to bear on objects at different distances, by convergence of the eyes.

4·10 The eyes converge on an object we examine, the images being brought to the foveas. In **a** we see the eyes converged to a near object, in **b** to one more distant. The angle of convergence is signalled to the brain as information of distance – serving as a range-finder.

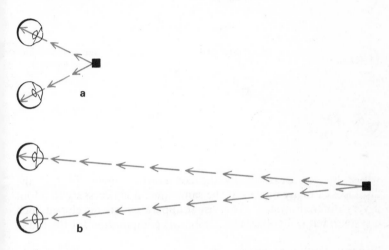

**Convergence, or range-finder, depth perception**

Figure 4·10 shows how the eyes pivot inwards for viewing near objects, and distance is signalled to the brain by this angle of convergence. This, however, is by no means the whole story.

A simple experiment shows that the convergence angle is used directly to signal distance. Figure 4·11a shows what happens if a pair of prisms of suitable angle are introduced to bend the light entering the eyes, so that they have to converge to bring distant objects on to the centre of the foveas. If the prisms are placed to *decrease* the angle of convergence (figure 4·11b) objects will appear nearer and larger; with prisms arranged to increase convergence objects appear further and smaller.* Depth perception is given in part by the angle of convergence of the eyes indicating distance, just as in a range-finder.

Now there is a serious limitation to range-finders: they can only indicate the distance of one object at a time; namely, the object

* The size changes however are complicated, because the total depth scale is shrunk or expanded by convergence. Cf. page 57.

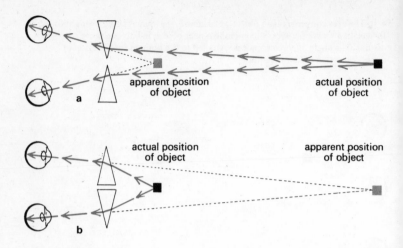

whose images are fused by the convergence angle. To find the distances of many objects at the same time, it is necessary to adopt a very different system. The visual apparatus has developed such a system, but it involves some elaborate computation for the brain.

### Disparity depth perception

The eyes are separated (by about 6·3 cm) and so receive somewhat different views. This can be seen quite clearly if first one eye then the other is held open. Any near object will appear to shift sideways in relation to more distant objects, and to rotate when each eye receives its view. This slight difference between the images is known as 'disparity.' It gives perception of depth by *stereoscopic vision*, which is employed in the stereoscope, a useful research tool.

The stereoscope is a simple instrument for presenting any two pictures separately to the two eyes. Normally these pictures are stereo pairs, made with a pair of cameras separated by the distance between the eyes, to give the disparity which the brain uses to give stereo vision. It makes it possible to study how the eyes use disparity for depth perception. (The stereoscope was a favourite Victorian toy, but unfortunately photographic subjects came to be chosen which, while ideally suited technically, met with such opposition that it was banned from the Victorian drawing room – a blow from which it has never recovered.)

4·11 The angle of convergence for a given distance can be changed by 53
interposing prisms. **a** shows increased, and **b** decreased, convergence. The effect
is to change the apparent size and distance of objects viewed through the prisms.
The change is not optical, but due to rescaling by the brain, its range-finder
giving it the wrong information. This is a useful experimental trick for establishing
the importance of convergence on perception of size and distance.

Stereo pictures may be presented reversed – the right eye
receiving the left eye's picture and *vice versa* – and then we may get
reversal of perceived depth. Generally speaking, depth reversal will
occur with pseudoscopic vision (as it is called) when this reversal
of depth would not grossly flout the familiar view. People's faces
will not reverse in depth (we do not see the nose as a hollow), but
the position of separate objects may well reverse in depth when the
eyes are switched.

It is quite a simple matter to reverse the eyes optically so that
the real world may be seen with the eyes interchanged. An instrument for doing this is called a pseudoscope (figure 4·12).

Stereo vision is only one of many ways in which we see depth,
and it only functions for comparatively near objects, after which
the difference between the images becomes so small that they become effectively identical. We are effectively one-eyed for distances
greater than perhaps 50 metres.

The brain must 'know' which eye is which, for otherwise depth
perception would be ambiguous. Also, reversal of the pictures in a
stereoscope, or a pseudoscope, would have no effect. But oddly
enough it is virtually impossible to *say* which eye is doing the
seeing. Although the eyes are fairly well identified for the depth
mechanism, this information is not available to consciousness.

If the pictures presented to the two eyes are quite different (or if
the difference between the viewing positions of an object is so
great that the corresponding features fall well outside the range
where fusion is possible) a curious and highly distinctive effect
occurs. Each eye in turn rejects its picture, or part of its picture,
so that continuous fluctuation takes place. Parts of each picture
are successively combined and rejected, in various ways. This is
known as 'retinal rivalry'. Rivalry also occurs if different colours
are presented to the two eyes, though fusion into mixture colours
can occur for short periods.

It is not known how the brain's computer for converting
differences between the images into depth works. It is possible,
however, to show the kind of information that the computer uses.

4·12 Switching the eyes with mirrors. (*Top*) A *pseudoscope* – gives reversed depth, but only when depth is somewhat ambiguous. (*Centre*) A *telestereoscope* – effectively increases the separation of the eyes. (*Bottom*) An *iconoscope* – reduces the effective distance apart of the eyes. These arrangements are all useful for studying convergence and disparity in depth perception.

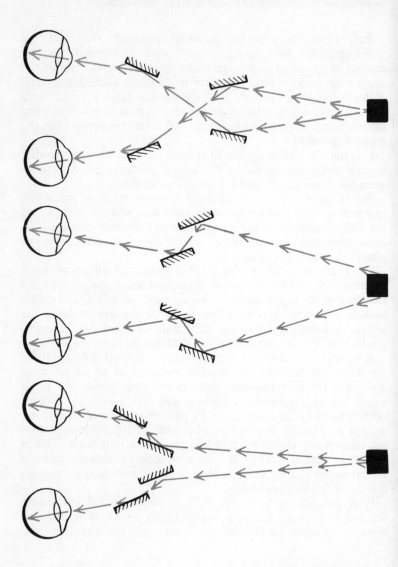

This may be done with a photographic trick, by placing the negative of one of a stereo pair on top of a transparent positive made from the negative of the other. Where the two pictures are identical no light will get through, but any difference allows light through, giving a picture of nothing but the differences. The kind of result one gets is shown in figure 4·13. It may be noted that almost all the information of the original picture is lost in this process. Such rejection of information would save the depth 'computer' a lot of work.

### The relation between convergence and stereo depth

We come now to a remarkable feature of stereo depth perception. There is a linkage between the two very different mechanisms I have described – (1) the convergence of the eyes serving as a *range finder*, and (2) the difference between the two images giving *disparity*. The angle of convergence adjusts the scale of the disparity system. When the eyes fixate a *distant* object, disparities between the images are accepted as representing *greater differences in depth*, than when the eyes are converged for near vision.

If this did not occur, distant objects would look closer together in depth than near objects of the same depth separation, for the disparity given by a depth difference is greater the nearer the objects. The linked mechanism compensating for this geometrical situation may be seen at work quite easily – by upsetting convergence while keeping the disparity the same. If the eyes are made to converge to infinity, with prisms, though near objects are being observed, they appear stretched out in depth. So we can see our convergence-disparity compensation system at work.

This trick for revealing compensatory mechanisms, by removing one of a pair of opposed signals or channels, is extremely useful. We will later adopt the same scheme to discover why the visual world remains stationary when the eyes move around (chapter 7), and for other problems. Perception involves many mechanisms using compensations, to avoid errors of various kinds, and this trick can generally be used to discover how they work.

It is often thought that stereoscopic information is used by the

4·13 This and the following two figures show how the brain uses disparity to judge depth. Below we see what happens when one of a stereo pair is subtracted, photographically, from the other photo of the pair. This *difference photograph* gives the disparity information – the differences between the images of the two eyes.

brain differently from other depth cues, such as perspective, in that most depth information is essentially ambiguous while the difference between the images of the two eyes can signal depth unambiguously. It is true that convergence and disparity are unambiguously related to distance – but it is *not* true that their information goes unchallenged. Stereoscopic signals are accepted as merely another source of distance information. They can be countermanded by other depth information, or by a high improbability of what they are signalling. This may be because, although stereoscopic information is not ambiguous, it is only reliable for near objects, since acuity is limited and the separation between the eyes is small. The effect of countering stereoscopic (and indeed simultaneously many other) sensory cues to depth by a high improbability is seen most dramatically by looking with both eyes and in normal lighting at the inside of a hollow mould of a face. The hollow face appears as a normal face, until it is viewed from very close when suddenly it is seen, truly, as hollow. This is illustrated in the author's *The Intelligent Eye*, page 131, with a stereo pair of photographs of a hollow face, and also a normal face. The hollow face appears as a normal face with correct stereo, and the normal face 'refuses' to appear hollow with the eyes reversed,

4·14 and 4·15 The difference picture is made up of the positive picture (*top*) and the
negative picture (*bottom*), which were placed one on top of the other to give 4·13.
It is possible that the brain does much the same thing, rejecting at that stage
all information except that indicating depth by disparity.

to give pseudoscopic stereo. This shows conclusively that stereo
does not *determine* depth – for it will not select a highly improbable
perception.

Until recently it has been assumed that stereoscopic vision always
functions by binocular comparison of contours: often the edges of
objects. In what has turned out to be an unusually important
experiment, Bela Julesz, of Bell Telephone Laboratories, has shown

4·16 These random patterns were computer-generated, with a lateral shift of each point in a central region of one of the patterns. When seen, one with each eye (using a stereoscope), this central region appears above the rest of the pattern – showing that the eyes perform a cross-correlation between the pair of patterns, to convert disparity (horizontal displacement) into perception of depth. Stereoscopic depth does not therefore depend upon contours, as had been thought before Julesz's experiments.

that contours are not needed. Julesz generated a pair of random dot patterns, with a computer, such that all were identical except that some regions were horizontally displaced, in one of the arrays. Viewed in a stereoscope, each eye received the same array of random dots except for the relative local horizontal displacements – which produced corresponding changes in apparent distance. Thus, stereo depth occurred without contours. Further, Julesz showed that the brain could synthesise (by cross-correlation) patterns shown only as random dot arrays, in which neither eye received contours, or a pattern.

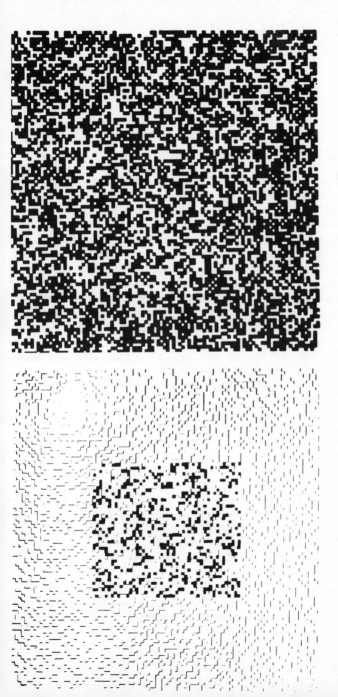

# 5 The brain

The brain is more complicated than a star and more mysterious. Looking, with imagination, back through the eyes to the brain mechanisms lying behind, we may there discover secrets as important as the secrets of the world perceived by the eye and brain.

It has not always been obvious that the brain is concerned with thinking, with memory, or with sensation. In the ancient world – including the great civilisations of Egypt and Mesopotamia – the brain was regarded as an unimportant organ. Thought and the emotions were attributed to the stomach, the liver and the gall bladder. Indeed, the echo lingers in modern speech, in such words as 'phlegmatic.' When the Egyptians embalmed their dead, they did not trouble to keep the brain (which was extracted through the left nostril) though the other organs were separately preserved, in special Canopic jars placed beside the sarcophagus. In death the brain is almost bloodless, so perhaps it seemed ill-suited to be the receptacle of the Vital Spirit. The active pulsing heart seemed to be the seat of life, warmth and feeling – not the cold grey silent brain, locked privily in its box of bone.

The vital role of the brain in control of the limbs, in speech and thought, sensation and experience, gradually became clear from the effects of accidents in which the brain was damaged. Later the effects of small tumours and gun shot wounds gave information which has been followed up and studied in great detail. The results of these studies are of the greatest importance to brain surgeons; for while some regions are comparatively safe, others must not be disturbed or the patient will die or suffer grievous loss.

The brain has been described as 'the only lump of matter we know from the inside.' From the outside, it is a pink-grey object, about the size of two clenched fists. Relevant parts are shown in figure 5·1. It is made up of the so-called 'white' and 'grey' matter, the white matter being the fibres connecting the cell bodies, forming the grey matter.

The brain has, in its evolution, grown up from the centre, which in man is concerned primarily with emotion. The surface – the *cortex* – is curiously convoluted. It is largely concerned with motor-

5·1 The brain, showing the visual part – the *area striata* – at the back (occipital cortex). Stimulation of small regions produces flashes of light in corresponding parts of the visual field. Stimulation of surrounding regions (visual association areas) produces more elaborate visual experiences.

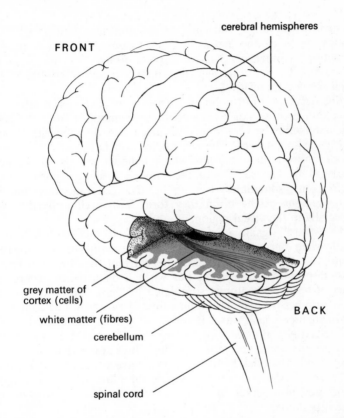

control of the limbs, and with the sense organs. It is possible to obtain maps of the association of regions of cortex with the sensation of touch on the skin – giving bizarre 'homunculi' as in figure 5·2. The sense of sight has its own region of cortex, as we shall see in a moment.

The nerve cells in the brain consist of *cell bodies* each having a long thin process – or *axon* – conducting impulses from the cell. The axons may be very long, sometimes extending from the brain down the spinal cord. The cell bodies also have many finer and shorter fibres, the *dendrites*, which conduct signals to the cell (figure 5·3). The cells, with their interconnecting dendrites and their axons, sometimes seem to be arranged randomly, but in some regions of the brain they form fairly well ordered rows, especially in the visual region.

The neural signals are in the form of electrical pulses, which occur when there is an alteration in the ion permeability of the cell membrane (figure 5·4). At rest, the centre of the fibre is negative with respect to the surface; but when a disturbance occurs, as when a retinal receptor is stimulated by light, the centre of the fibre becomes positive, initiating a flow of current which continues down the nerve as a wave. It travels very much more slowly than does electricity along a wire: in large fibres it travels at about 100 metres per second, and in the smallest fibres at less than one metre per second. The thick high-speed fibres have a special fatty coating – the *myelin sheath* – which insulates the fibres from their neighbours and also serves to increase the rate of conduction of the action potential.

Nerves are joined by synapses, which are junctions where chemicals are released which serve as triggers. Most, and perhaps all neurones have both excitatory and inhibitory synapses which act as switches.

There are many sophisticated techniques for studying the nervous system. Electrical activity of individual cells, or groups of cells, may be recorded; regions may be stimulated electrically to evoke not only responses but even – in patients undergoing brain

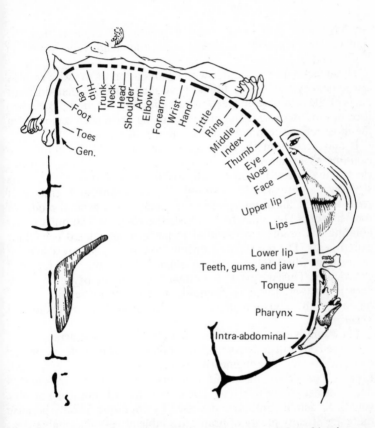

5·2 A 'homunculus' – a graphic representation showing how much of the cortex is devoted to sensation from various regions of the body. Note the huge thumb. Different animals have very different 'homunculi', corresponding to the sensory importance of the various parts of the body.

Leg
Hip
Trunk
Neck
Head
Shoulder
Arm
Elbow
Forearm
Wrist
Hand
Little
Ring
Middle
Index
Thumb
Eye
Nose
Face
Upper lip
Lips
Lower lip
Teeth, gums, and jaw
Tongue
Pharynx
Intra-abdominal
Foot
Toes
Gen.

operations – sensations. The effects of loss of regions of brain may be discovered, resulting behaviour changes being related to the regions of damage. The effects of drugs or chemicals applied directly to the surface of the brain may be investigated; this is becoming an important area of research both to establish that new drugs do not have unpleasant psychological side effects, and as a direct technique for deliberately changing the state of the brain.

An advantage over destruction of regions of brain is that the changes are generally reversible, and may readily be varied in degree and in kind.

These techniques, together with examination of the way regions are joined by bundles of fibres, have made it clear that different parts of the brain are engaged in very different functions. But when it comes to discovering the processes going on in each region, even the most refined techniques look rather crude.

It may seem that the most direct way to study the brain is to examine its structure, and stimulate it and record from it. But like electronic devices, it is not at all easy to see how it works from its structure; and the results of stimulation, recording, and removal of parts are difficult to interpret in the absence of a general model of how it works. In order to establish the results of stimulating or ablating the brain, it is essential to perform associated behaviour experiments. The results of recording from brain cells are also most interesting when there is some related behaviour, or reported experience. This means that animal and human psychology are very important, for it is essential to relate brain activity to behaviour, and this involves specially designed psychological experiments.

The brain is, of course, an immensely complicated arrangement of nerve cells but it is somewhat similar to man-made electronic devices, so general engineering considerations can be helpful. Like a computer, the brain accepts information, and makes decisions according to the available information; but it is not very similar to actual computers designed by engineers, if only because there are already plenty of brains available at very reasonable cost, and they are easy to make by a well-proved method, so that computers are designed to be different.

It is easier to make a machine to solve mathematical or logical problems – to handle symbols according to rules – than to see. The problem of making machines to recognise patterns has been solved in various ways for restricted ranges of patterns, but so far there is no neat solution, and no machine comes anywhere

5·3 A nerve cell. The cell body has a long axon, insulated by its myelin sheath, 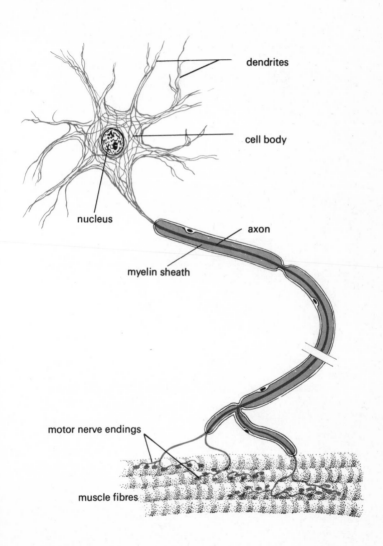often sending control signals to muscle. The cell body accepts information from the many fine dendrites, some of which tend to make the cell fire, while others inhibit firing. The system is a simple computer element. The inter-connected elements serve to control activity and handle information for perception.

dendrites

cell body

nucleus

axon

myelin sheath

motor nerve endings

muscle fibres

5·4 Mechanism of electrical conduction in nerve. Hodgkin, Huxley and Katz have discovered that sodium ions pass to the inside of the fibre, converting its standing negative charge to positive. Potassium ions leak out, restoring the resting potential. This can happen up to a thousand times a second, transmitting spikes of potential which run along the nerve as the signals by which we know the world, and command the muscles.

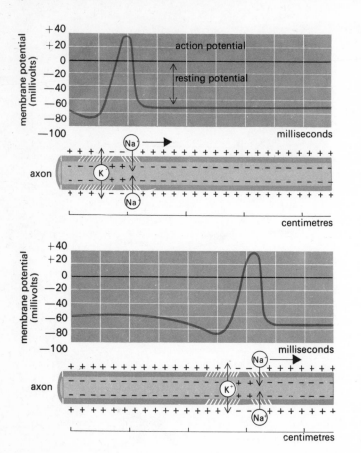

near the human perceptual system in range or speed. It is partly for this reason that detailed study of human perception is important. Finding out what we can of human perception may suggest ways in which perception can be achieved by machines. This would be useful for many purposes – from the reading of docu⁻ments and books to the exploration of space by robots.

One of the difficulties in understanding the function of the brain is that it is like nothing so much as a lump of porridge. With mechanical systems, it is usually possible to make a good guess at function by considering the structure of the parts, and this is true of much of the body. The bones of the limbs are *seen* to be levers. The position of attachment of the muscles clearly determines their function.

Mechanical and optical systems have parts whose shapes are closely related to their function, which makes it possible to deduce, or at least guess, their function from their shape. It was possible for Kepler to guess that a structure in the eye, (called at that time the 'crystalline') is in fact a lens from its shape. It was a rather simple matter for Scheiner to discover the image, because he knew where to look. But unfortunately the brain presents a far more difficult problem, if only because the physical arrangement of its parts and their shapes is rather unimportant to their function. When function is not reflected in structure we cannot deduce function by simply looking. We must try to deduce function from design principles of the system.

The electrical activity recorded by physiologists is extremely important, but unfortunately it is very difficult to get detailed information of the separate activity of more than a few cells at a time, or to 'infer' its functions.

Design principles may be suggested by engineering considerations. If a given possible engineering design has certain limitations, and experiments on animals or human beings show they have similar limitations, then such experiments may confirm hypotheses perhaps culled originally from engineering. In particular, perceptual experiments can be important tools for discovering or testing models of brain function. Looking out through the eyes, the brain sees the world – by looking in through the eyes via suitable experiments we can see the brain as a functional system limited by physical, engineering, considerations.

## The visual regions of the brain

The neural system responsible for vision starts with the retinas. These, as we have seen, are essentially outgrowths of the brain, containing typical brain cells as well as specialised light-sensitive detectors. The retinas are effectively divided vertically down the middle, the fibres from the outer sides going to the same side of the back of the brain, while the fibres from the inner, nasal, sides of the retinas cross just behind the eyes – at the *optic chiasma* – and go to the opposite sides of the back of the brain (figure 5·5). This visual region at the back of the brain is known as the *area striata*, from its appearance, the cells being arranged in rows (*frontispiece*).

The brain as a whole is divided down the middle, forming two hemispheres, which are really more-or-less complete brains, joined by a massive bundle of fibres the *corpus callosum*, and the smaller *optic chiasma*. On their way from the chiasma, the optic tract passes through a relay station in each hemisphere, the *lateral geniculate body*.

The central region of *area striata* is known as the 'visual projection area.' When a small part is stimulated a human patient reports a flash of light. Upon a slight change of position of the stimulating electrode, a flash is seen in another part of the visual field. It thus seems there is a spatial representation of the retinas upon the visual cortex. Stimulation of surrounding regions of the striate area also gives visual sensations, but instead of flashes of light the sensations are more elaborate. Brilliant coloured balloons may be seen floating up in an infinite sky. Further away, stimulation may elicit visual memories, even complete scenes coming vividly before the eyes.

Among the most exciting of recent discoveries, is the finding of

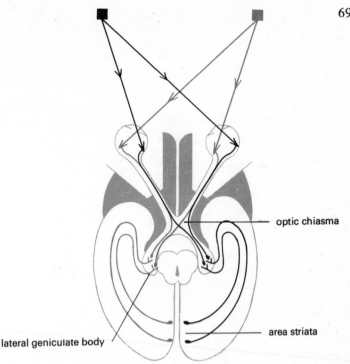

optic chiasma

lateral geniculate body

area striata

two American physiologists, D. Hubel and T. Wiesel, who recorded activity from single cells of the visual area of the cat's brain while presenting its eyes with simple visual shapes. These were generally bars of light, projected by a slide projector on a screen in front of the cat. Hubel and Wiesel found that some cells were only active when the bar of light was presented to the cat at a certain angle. At that particular angle the brain cell would fire, with long bursts of impulses, while at other angles it was 'silent.' Different cells would respond to different angles. Cells deeper in the brain responded to more generalised characteristics, and would respond to these characteristics no matter which part of the retina was stimulated by the light. Other cells responded only to movement, and movement in only a single direction (figure 5·6). These findings are of the greatest importance, for they show that there are analysing mechanisms in the brain, selecting certain features of objects.

We do have 'mental pictures', but this should not suggest that

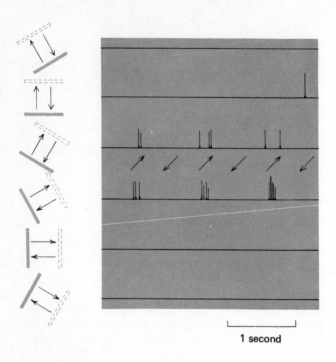

5·6 Hubel and Wiesel's discovery that selected single brain cells (in the cat) fire with movement at the eye in a certain direction. The arrows show various directions of movement of a bar of light presented to the eyes. The electrical record shows that this particular cell fires only for one direction of movement.

1 second

there are corresponding electrical pictures in the brain, for things can be represented in symbols – but symbols will generally be very different from the things represented. The notion of brain pictures is conceptually dangerous. It is apt to suggest that these supposed pictures are themselves seen with a kind of inner eye – involving another picture, and another eye . . . and so on.

In any case, it is not possible to suppose that sounds and smells and colours are represented by pictures in the brain – they *must* be coded in some other form. There is every reason to believe that

5·7 Hubel and Wiesel's records from single cells in the visual cortex of the cat. A line (shown on the left) was presented to the cat at various orientations. A single cell in the brain fires only at a certain orientation. This is shown by the spikes of the electrical records.

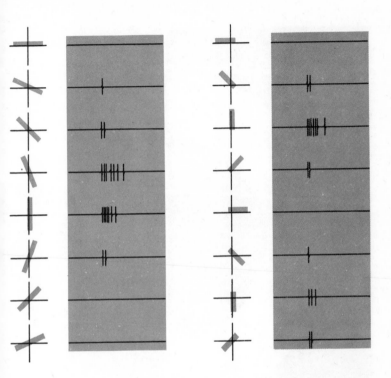

retinal patterns are represented by coded combinations of cell activity. Hubel and Wiesel, and other electrophysiologists, are now beginning to discover the basic symbols of the code.

It is now being shown that while primary visual pattern information is represented at the surface of the visual cortex, deeper down the representation is more general, and related to other sensory and probably also memory information. The visual cortex is organised not only in the clearly visible layers, parallel with its surface, but also in functional 'columns' penetrating the layers down which information from many sources is collected to give, finally, perception.

6·1 Simultaneous contrast. The part of the grey ring seen against the black appears somewhat lighter than the rest, seen against white.
This effect is enhanced if a fine thread is placed across the ring along the black–white junction.

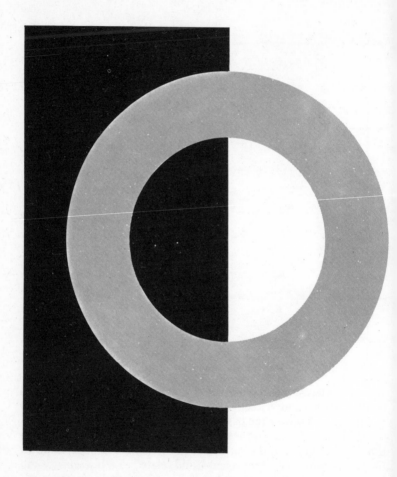

# 6 Seeing brightness

There is supposed to be a primitive tribe of cattle breeders who have no word for green in their language, but have six words for different shades of red – specialists in all fields adopt special meanings for their own use. Before embarking on a discussion of brightness and colour, we should stop for a moment to sharpen some words – as a carpenter might stop to sharpen his chisels before attempting delicate work.

We speak of *intensity* of light entering the eye, giving rise to *brightness*. Intensity is the physical energy of the light, which may be measured by various kinds of photometer, including the familiar photographer's exposure meter. Brightness is an experience. We believe we know what another person means when he says 'what a bright day!' He means not only that he could take photographs with a slow film in his camera, but also that he experiences a dazzling sensation. This sensation is roughly, but only roughly, related to the intensity of the light entering the eyes.

When talking about colour vision, we do not generally talk of colours', but rather of 'hues'. This is simply to avoid the difficulty that 'colours' are apt to mean sensations to which we can give a specific name, such as 'red' or 'blue'. We thus speak technically of 'spectral hues' rather than 'spectral colours', but this is not always necessary. The intensity-brightness distinction is far more important.

Another important distinction to be made is *colour as a sensation* and *colour as a wavelength* (or set of wavelengths) of the light entering the eye. Strictly speaking, light itself is not coloured: it gives rise to sensations of brightness and colour, but only in conjunction with a suitable eye and nervous system. The technical language is somewhat confused on this matter: we do speak sometimes of 'coloured light,' such as 'yellow light', but this is loose. It should be taken to mean: light which generally gives rise to a sensation, described by most people as 'yellow'.

Without attempting to explain how physical intensities and wavelengths of radiation give rise to different sensations (and ultimately we do not know the answer) we should realise quite clearly that without life there would be no brightness and no colour. Before life came all was silent though the mountains toppled.

The simplest of the visual sensations is brightness. It is impossible to describe the sensation. A blind man knows nothing of it, and yet to the rest of us reality is made up of brightness and of colour. The opposed sensation of blackness is as powerful – we speak of a 'solid wall of blackness pressing in on us' – but to the blind this also means nothing. The sensation given to us by absence of light is blackness: but the blind are visually asleep, dead. We come nearest to picturing the world of the blind, who have no brightness and no black, by thinking of the region behind our heads. We do not experience blackness behind us: we experience nothing, and this is very different.

Brightness is not just a simple matter of the intensity of light striking the retina. The brightness given by a given intensity depends upon the state of adaptation of the eye, and also upon various complicated conditions determining the contrast of objects or patches of light. In other words, brightness is a function not only of the intensity of light falling on a given region of the retina at a certain time; but also of the intensity of the light that the retina has been subject to in the recent past, and of the intensities of light falling on other regions of the retina.

## Dark-light adaptation

If the eyes are kept in darkness for some time, they grow more sensitive and a given light will look brighter. This so-called dark adaptation takes place in the first few minutes of darkness. The rod and cone receptor cells adapt at different rates: cone-adaptation is completed in about seven minutes, while rod-adaptation continues for an hour or more. This is shown in figure 6·2, where it will be seen that there are really two adaptation curves – one for the rods the other for the cones. It is as if we have not one, but two retinas, lying inter-mingled in the eye.

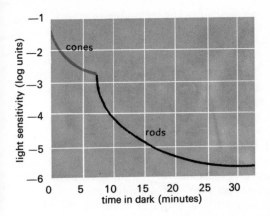

6·2 Increase in sensitivity of the eye in the dark, known as *dark adaptation*. The *red* curve shows how the cone cells adapt, while the *black* curve shows rod adaptation, which is slower and proceeds to greater sensitivity. In dim light only the rods are functional, while they are probably inhibited in brighter light used by the active cones.

The mechanisms of dark-adaptation are beginning to be understood in detail, largely through the ingenious and technically brilliant experiments of the British physiologist W. A. H. Rushton. It was suggested many years ago that adaptation is due to regeneration of the visual pigments of the eye bleached by light – this bleaching in some unknown way stimulating the receptors to give the electrical signals to the optic nerve. The photochemical rhodopsin was extracted from the frog's eye, and its density to light measured during bleaching and regeneration, and compared with human dark-adaptation curves. The two curves are shown together in figure 6·4, and indeed they do correspond very closely, suggesting a strong connection between the photochemistry of rhodopsin and the changing sensitivity of the rod eye. It would also seem that brightness must be related to the amount of photochemical present to be bleached. What Rushton has now done is to measure directly the density of the photochemical in the living eye, during adaptation to darkness or to any coloured light he may wish to use during the experiment. The technique is, essentially, to shine a brief flash of light into the eye and to measure the amount of light reflected from it, with a very sensitive photocell. At first it seemed impossible to do this for the human eye because so little light remains to be reflected, after the almost complete absorption by the photochemicals and the black pigment lying behind the receptors; and so a cat's eye was used, the reflecting layer at the back, the tapetum, serving as a mirror to reflect light into the photocell. The method worked with the cat's eye, and Rushton then succeeded in refining it to make it sufficiently sensitive to detect and measure the very feeble light reflected from the human eye. He finds that there is bleaching of the photochemicals with adaptation, the relation between the stimulus energy and the amount of photochemical which is bleached being logarithmic. He has now detected the colour-sensitive pigments in this way.

## Contrast

Another factor which affects brightness is the intensity of surrounding areas. A given region generally looks brighter if its surroundings are dark, and a given colour looks more intense if it is surrounded by its complementary colour. This is no doubt related to the cross-connections between the receptors. Contrast enhancement seems to be tied up with the general importance of borders in perception. It seems that it is primarily the existence of borders which are signalled to the brain, while regions of constant intensity do not need much information. The visual system extrapolates between borders, which no doubt saves a lot of information-handling by the peripheral parts of the system, though at the cost of some complexity further up in the brain. This probably starts with *lateral inhibition*. Although the phenomena of contrast and enhancement of borders are no doubt mainly due to retinal mechanisms, there do seem to be more central contributions. This is brought out in figure 6·1 which shows quite marked contrast; the even grey ring appears lighter where it lies against the dark background than where it lies against the white. But this effect is considerably more marked when a fine thread is placed across the ring continuing the division of the background; the contrast is greater when the figure is interpreted as two separate halves than when it is regarded as all one figure. This suggests that central brain factors play a part.

Something of the subtlety of the human brightness system is shown by Fechner's Paradox. This is as follows. Present the eye with a small, fairly bright source: it will look a certain brightness, and the pupil will close to a certain size when the light is switched on. Now add a second, dimmer light. This is placed some way from the first, so that a different region of retina is stimulated. What happens? Although the total intensity has increased with the addition of the second light, the pupil does not close further as one might expect: rather it opens, to correspond to an intensity between the first and the second light. It is evidently set not by the *total*, but by the *average* illumination. Nobody knows how the retina does it.

Try shutting one eye, and noting any change in brightness. There is practically no difference whether one or two eyes receive the light. This, however, is not so when small dim lights are viewed in surrounding darkness: they *do* look considerably brighter with two eyes than with one. This phenomenon is not understood.

Brightness is a function of colour. If we shine lights of different colours but the same intensity into the eyes, the colours at the middle of the spectrum will look brighter than those at the ends. This is shown in figure 6·5, the curve being known as the *spectral luminosity curve*. This is of some practical importance, for if a distress signal light is to be clearly visible, it should be of a colour to which the eye is maximally sensitive – in the middle of the spectrum. The matter is complicated by the fact that the sensitivity curves for rods and cones are somewhat different. They are similar in general shape, but the cones are most sensitive to yellow, while the rods are most sensitive to green. (For this reason, it is a good idea to paint the walls of photographic darkrooms green, since the eye then gets its most effective light, whilst the film is relatively unaffected).

The luminosity curve tells us nothing much about colour vision. It is sensitivity to light plotted against wavelength of light, but with no reference to the colours seen at each wavelength. Animals without colour vision show a similar luminosity curve.

It seems that although there are photochemical changes associated with adaptation to light, there are several additional mechanisms at work, these being not photochemical but neural. In particular, as the eye becomes dark-adapted, it trades its acuity in space and in time for increase in sensitivity. With dark adaptation ability to make out fine detail is lost. This is no simple matter, but it is in part due to the retina integrating energy over a greater area – over a greater number of receptors. There is also an increase in the time over which energy can be integrated as the eye dark-adapts.

The trading of temporal discrimination for sensitivity with dark adaptation is most elegantly, if somewhat indirectly, observed in a curious and dramatic phenomenon known as the *Pulfrich Pendulum Effect*. Not least remarkable about this effect is its discovery, for the effect cannot be seen without two functional eyes, and yet its discoverer was blind in one eye! The experiment is worth trying out. Take a length of string, and a weight for a bob to make a pendulum one metre long. Swing the pendulum in a straight arc normal to the line of sight. View the oscillating bob with both eyes, but cover one with a dark, though not opaque, glass. (Half a pair of sun glasses is quite suitable, or some exposed film). It will be found that the bob does not appear to swing in a straight arc, but to *describe an ellipse*. The ellipse may be extremely eccentric – indeed the major axis can lie *along* the line of sight, though the bob is actually swinging straight across the line of sight.

Now what causes this strange effect? By reducing the light, the dark glass has dark-adapted its eye. This adaptation produces a delay in the message reaching the brain from this eye, though the other is unaffected. The delay causes the affected eye to see the bob slightly in the past, and as the bob speeds up in the middle of its swing, this delay becomes more important, for the eye with the filter sees it in a position further and further behind the position signalled to the brain by the unaffected eye. This difference of effective position generates an ellipse lying in depth; for the brain it is exactly as though the bob were in fact swinging in an ellipse. This is shown in figure 6·3. It seems that increased delay with dark-adaptation is associated with increase in temporal integrating time – as when a photographer uses a longer exposure in dim light. We see this directly by noting the increasing length of the 'comet's tail' of a moving firework, as dark-adaptation increases in the dark.

Both the increase in the delay of messages from the retina to the brain, and the increase in the integrating time which this allows, have some practical significance. The retinal delay produces a lengthening of reaction-time in drivers in dim light, and the increased integrating time makes precise localisation of moving objects more difficult. Games cannot be played so well: the umpire calls 'Cease play for poor light' long before the spectators think it right to bow before the setting sun.

## The eye's sensitivity to light

As intensity of light is increased the rate of firing of the receptors increases, intensity being signalled by the rate of firing. Unfortunately it is not possible to record the electrical activity in the receptors of a vertebrate eye because the retina is 'inside out' so that an electrode cannot reach them without doing extensive damage. By the time the optic nerve is reached the signals have been complicated by the cross-connections of the layers of nerve cells in the retina. There is however an eye – that of a living fossil, the Horse Shoe Crab, *Limulus*, found on the eastern seaboard of the United States – in which the receptors are connected directly to separate nerve fibres. The individual pathways of the ancient

6·3 The Pulfrich Pendulum. A pendulum swinging in a straight arc across the line of sight is viewed with a dark glass over one eye, both eyes being open. It appears to swing in an ellipse. This is due to the signals from the eye which is partly dark adapted by the glass being delayed. The increasing effective separation for the two eyes towards the middle of the swing is interpreted as a difference in distance, generating an ellipse.

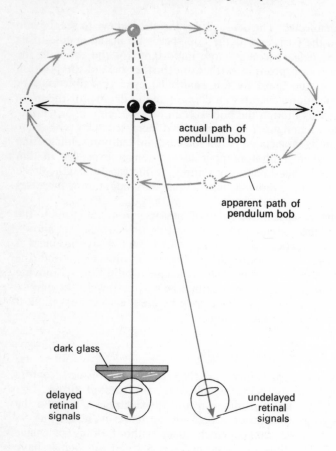

actual path of
pendulum bob

apparent path of
pendulum bob

dark glass

delayed
retinal
signals

undelayed
retinal
signals

*Limulus* eye have turned out to be most useful, though this could hardly have been anticipated in their original design. Figure 6·6 shows the electrical activity in a nerve fibre of a *Limulus* eye. In the receptors of *Limulus*, the rate of firing of a receptor has been found to be approximately logarithmically related to intensity of light. This is shown in figure 6·8.

The first record (figure 6·6) shows a low rate of firing after the eye has been in the dark for one minute. The other record (figure 6·7) shows the firing rate increasing as the eye has been in the dark for a longer time. This corresponds to our own experience of increasing brightness after being in the dark.

What happens when we look at a very faint light in an otherwise dark room? One might imagine that in the absence of light, there is no activity reaching the brain, and when there is any light at all the retina signals its presence, and we see the light. But it is not quite so simple. In the total absence of light, the retina and optic nerve are not entirely free of activity. There is always some residual neural activity reaching the brain, even when there is no stimulation of the eye by light. This is known from direct recording of the activity of the optic nerve in the fully dark-adapted cat's eye, and we have very strong reasons for believing that the same is true for the human and all other eyes.

This matter of a continuous background of random activity is of great importance. The eye is remarkably sensitive – we can see a flash of light so feeble that it is difficult to detect with any man-made instrument – but the eye would be still more sensitive if it were not for the background activity of the visual system, which imposes a continuous problem for the brain.

Imagine some neural pulses arriving at the brain: are they due to light entering the eye, or are they merely spontaneous 'noise' in the system? The brain's problem is to 'decide' whether neural activity is representing outside events, or whether it is mere 'noise' which should be ignored. This is a situation very familiar to the communications engineer, for all sensitive detectors are subject to random-noise degenerating signals, which always limits the

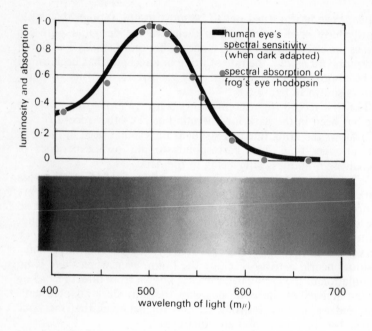

6·4 The chemical basis of vision. The curve in black shows the sensitivity of the (dark adapted) human eye to various wavelengths of light. The red dots show the amount of light over the same range of wavelengths absorbed by the photochemical rhodopsin in the frog's eye. The curves are substantially the same, indicating that the human eye, when dark adapted, functions by absorption of light by the same photochemical.

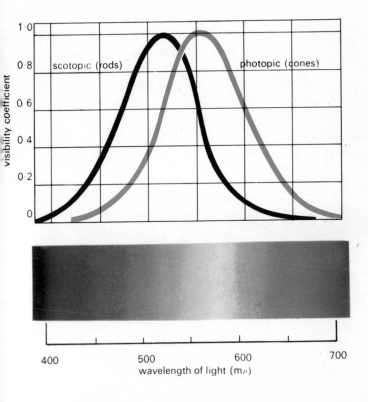

6·5 This shows how the sensitivity of the eye to various wavelengths of the spectrum is different when the eye is *light adapted*. The black curve shows the dark adapted sensitivity, while the red curve shows that this shifts along the spectrum with light adaptation, when the cones take over from the rods. This is known as the *Purkinje shift*.

6·6 (*Top*) This shows the electrical activity, recorded on an oscilloscope, of a single fibre of the optic nerve of *Limulus* for three intensities of light. The rate of firing increases roughly in proportion to the log. of the intensity.
6·7 (*Bottom*) The rate of firing after various durations of darkness. With increasing dark adaptation the rate increases, corresponding to increase in apparent brightness though the actual intensity of the light is the same.

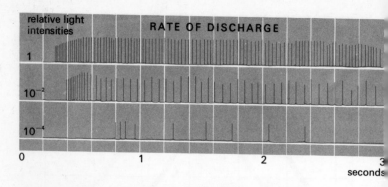

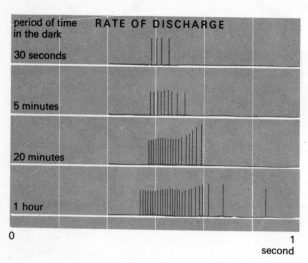

6·8 This is derived from the kind of records shown in 6·6 and 6·7. The rate of       85
firing is plotted against the log. of the intensity, giving approximately
a straight line, showing a logarithmic relation between rate of firing and
intensity for constant adaptation.

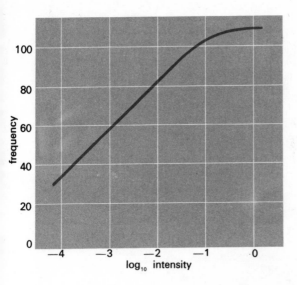

sensitivity of the detector. There are ways of reducing the harmful
effects of noise; these are applied with good effect by radio
astronomers, and in the detecting of small earth tremors – noise
masks the radio sources in space and the earth just as it masks and
confuses weak visual signals. The eye adopts certain measures to
reduce the effects of noise, notably increasing the duration over
which signals are integrated, which we saw reflected in the Pulfrich
effect, and by demanding several confirming signals from separate
receptors serving as independent witnesses.

One of the oldest laws in experimental psychology is Weber's
Law. This states that the smallest difference in intensity which can
be detected is directly proportional to the background intensity.
For example: if we light a candle in a brightly lit room, its effect is
scarcely noticeable, but if the room be dim to start with – say, lit
by just a few other candles – then the added candle makes a

6·9 Weber's Law ($\Delta I/I = C$). Plotting $\Delta I$ against $I$, gives a horizontal straight line over a wide range of $I$, but the law breaks down at low intensities, when $\Delta I/I$ must be raised for detection. Plotting $\Delta I$ against $I$ gives a substantially straight line down to small values of $I$, indicating a hidden constant k in the denominator. We may thus write the Law as $\Delta I/I + k = C$, where k appears to be related to neural noise level. These curves show the breakdown at low intensities.

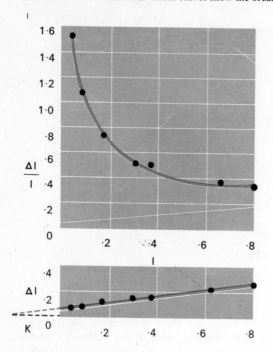

marked difference. In fact we can detect a change in intensity of about one per cent of the background illumination. This is written

$$\frac{\Delta I}{I} = \text{Constant}$$ ($\Delta$ meaning the small incremental intensity over the background intensity, $I$). Now this law holds fairly well over a wide range of background intensity, $I$, but it breaks down for low intensities. This may be seen in figure 6·9 where, if Weber's Law did hold down to zero intensity, we would have a horizontal straight line, indicating invariance of the just detectable differential

6·10 This attempts to show the statistical problem presented to the brain due to the random firing of nerves. When the signal field $(I + \Delta I)$ is being discriminated from its dimmer background ($I$) the pulse rates are not always different, but are so distributed as in the graph. So we may see a 'light' due to 'noise', or miss it when the rate is lower than average. The brain demands a significant difference before accepting neural activity as a signal.

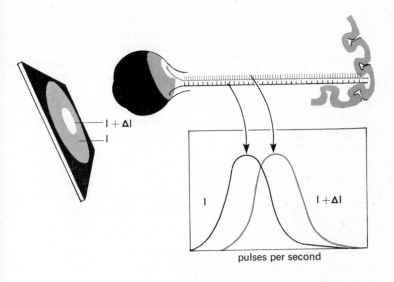

pulses per second

intensity $\dfrac{\Delta I}{I}$ over all values of $I$. In fact we get the full line shown in this graph, indicating a marked rise in $\dfrac{\Delta I}{I}$ as the background intensity becomes small. This breakdown is largely explained if we take into account the residual firing of the retinal cells in the absence of light. The residual activity is to the brain exactly equivalent to a more or less constant dim light added to the background. We may estimate its value by extrapolating back past the origin, and reading off the $y$-axis of the graph. This gives it in terms of an equivalent light intensity we may call $k$.

This hidden constant, $k$, can be attributed to the 'noise' of the retina. There is evidence that this internal noise of the visual system increases with age: the increased noise level is indeed no doubt partly responsible for the gradual loss of all visual discriminations with ageing. Increased noise may also affect motor control and memory.

The idea that discrimination is limited by noise in the nervous system has far-reaching consequences. It suggests that the old idea of a *threshold* intensity, beyond which stimuli need to go before they have any effect on the nervous system, is wrong. We now think of any stimulus as having an effect on the nervous system, but only being accepted as a signal of an outside event when the neural activity is unlikely to be merely a chance increase in the noise level. The situation may be represented as in figure 6·10. This shows a patch of light serving as a background ($I$) on which is added light ($\Delta I$) being detected. These two intensities of light give rise to statistically distributed neural impulse rates. The problem for the brain is to 'decide' when a given increase is merely chance, and when it is due to the increased intensity of the signal. If the brain accepted *any* increase from the average activity, then we would 'see' flashes of light not in fact present half the time. We thus reach the idea that a significant difference is demanded before neural activity is accepted as representing a signal. The smallest difference ($\Delta I$) we can see is determined not simply by the sensitivity of the receptors of the retina, but also by the difference in neural pulse rate demanded for acceptance as a signal.

Sometimes we do see flashes which are not there. These are evidently due to the noise exceeding the demanded significance level, and this is bound to happen on occasions.

The choice of the level above which activity is accepted is a matter of trading reliability for sensitivity. There is evidence that this level is to some extent variable, and depends on our 'set' When we are particularly careful, more information is demanded and sensitivity suffers.

This picture of intensity discrimination applies throughout the nervous system. It applies not only to differences between intensities but also to the absolute limit of detection against darkness, for the absolute threshold is determined by the smallest signal which can be reliably detected against the random background of the neural noise present in the brain though no light enters the eye.

## 'Seeing' with the skin

It has recently been claimed, by Paul Bach-y-Rita, that patterns of touch, given by an array of electrically driven probes placed on the surface of the skin, can give perception of external objects, as though the skin were serving as a tactile retina. A television camera is connected to the touch probes, so that light and dark are coded into pressure on each probe. After some hours of practice – and provided the subject can move the camera about under his own control – the subject ceases to feel the contact of the probes on his skin (generally his back) and the changing touch patterns become interpreted as external objects.

The stages of learning to 'see' through the skin with this apparatus seem remarkably similar to the stages by which people born blind and given operations to the eyes (pages 191–200) come to relate their images to objects, allowing them to see.

7·1 Herman von Helmholtz (1821–94), the greatest figure in the experimental study of vision. His *Physiological Optics* is still the most important work on the subject; indeed, disappointingly little has been added since.

# 7 Seeing movement

Detection of movement is essential to survival. From the animals lowest on the evolutionary scale to man, moving objects are likely to be either dangerous or potential food, and so rapid appropriate action is demanded, while stationary objects can generally be ignored. Indeed it now seems that it is only the eyes of the highest animals which can signal anything to the brain in the absence of movement.

Something of the evolutionary development of the eye, from movement to shape perception, can be seen embalmed in the human retina. The edge of the retina is sensitive only to movement. This may be seen by getting someone to wave an object around at the side of the visual field, where only the edge of the retina is stimulated. It will be found that the movement and the direction of movement is seen, but it is impossible to identify the object. When the movement stops, the object becomes invisible. This is as close as we can come to experiencing primitive perception. The very extreme edge of the retina is even more primitive: when stimulated by movement we experience nothing, but a reflex is initiated which rotates the eye to bring the moving object into central vision, so that the highly developed foveal region with its associated central neural network is brought into play for identifying the object. The edge of the retina is thus an early-warning device, used to rotate the eyes to aim the object-recognition part of the system on to objects likely to be friend or foe rather than neutral.

Those eyes, like our own, which move in the head can give information of movement in two distinct ways. When the eye remains stationary, the image of a moving object will run across the receptors and give rise to velocity signals from the retinas: but when the eyes follow a moving object, the images remain more or less stationary upon the retinas, and so *they* cannot signal movement, *but we still see the movement of the object*. If the object is viewed against a fixed background, there may be velocity signals from the background, which now sweep across the retinas as the eyes follow the moving object, *but we still see movement even when there is no background*. This can be demonstrated with a simple experiment. Ask someone to wave a lighted cigarette around slowly in a dark room; and follow it with the eyes. The movement of the cigarette is seen although there is no image moving across the retinas. Evidently, the rotation of the eyes in the head can give perception of movement, and fairly accurate estimates of velocity, in the absence of movement signals from the retinas.

There are, then, two movement systems, and we name them (a) the *image/retina* system, and (b) the *eye/head* system (figure 7·2). (These names follow those used in gunnery, where similar considerations apply when guns are aimed from the moving platform of a ship. The gun turret may be stationary or following, but movement of the target can be detected in either case.)

We may now take a look at the image/retina system, and then see how the two systems work in collaboration.

### The image retina movement system

It is found, by recording the electrical activity from the retinas of animals, that there are various kinds of receptors, almost all signalling only changes of illumination and very few giving a continuous signal to a steady light. Some signal when a light is switched on, others when it is switched off, while others again signal when it is switched on or off. Those various kinds are named, appropriately enough, 'on,' 'off,' and 'on-off' receptors. It seems that these receptors, sensitive only to change of illumination, are responsible for signalling movement, and that *all eyes are primarily detectors of movement*. The receptors signalling only changes will respond to the leading and trailing edges of images, but will not signal the presence of stationary images unless the eyes are in movement.

By placing fine wires (electrodes) in the retinas of excised frogs' eyes, it has been found that analysis of the receptor activity takes place in the retina before the brain is reached. A paper charmingly titled: 'What the Frog's Eye Tells the Frog's Brain' by Lettvin, Maturana, McCulloch and Pitts, of the Research Laboratory of Electronics at MIT, describes a retinal 'bug detector' and three

7·2 **a** The image/retina system: the image of a moving object runs along the retina when the eyes are held still, giving information of movement through sequential firing of the receptors in its path. **b** The eye/head movement system: when the eye follows a moving object the image remains stationary upon the retina, but we still see the movement. The two systems can sometimes disagree, giving curious illusions.

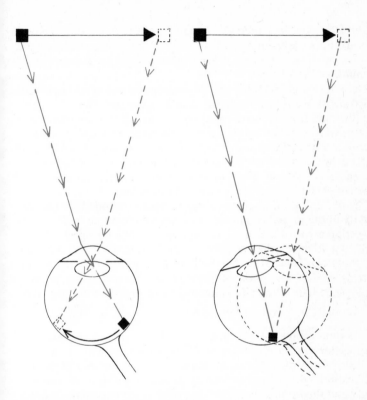

classes of fibres sending different kinds of information to the brain. The 'bug detector' elicits a reflex movement of the tongue when a small shadow, corresponding to a fly, falls on the retina, and so the retina is serving in this respect as a brain. In addition to this system, which responds essentially to curved lines, they find:

1 Fibres responding only to sharply defined boundaries between objects.
2 Fibres responding only to changes in the distribution of light.
3 Fibres responding only to a general dimming of illumination, such as might be caused by the shadow of a bird of prey.

The frog's eye signals only changing light patterns and moving curved edges; everything else is ignored and never reaches the brain. The frog's visual world is thus limited to movement of certain kinds of objects.

The physiologists Hubel and Wiesel have conducted important experiments recording from the visual region of the cat's brain, and they find that there are some single cells which respond only to movement across the retina, and to movement in only a certain direction. Figure 5·6 shows actual records of the activity of selected single cells from the cat's brain during stimulation of the eye by movements of various kinds, and it will be seen that some cells are sensitive only to movement in certain directions.

The physiological discovery that movement is coded into neural activity in the retina, or immediately behind the retina in the visual projection areas of the brain, is important in many respects; but in particular it shows that *velocity can be perceived without involving an estimate of time*. It is, however, often assumed that the neural systems giving perception of velocity must resort to an internal 'biological clock.' Velocity is defined in physics as the time taken for an object to travel a given distance $\left(v = \frac{d}{t}\right)$. It is then assumed that a time estimate is always required to estimate velocity. But the speedometer of a car has no clock associated with it. A clock is needed for calibrating such an instrument in the first place, but once calibrated it will give velocity measures without the use of a clock, and the same is evidently true of the eye. The image running across the retina sequentially fires the receptors, and the faster the image travels, up to a limit, the greater the velocity signal this gives. Analogies with other velocity detectors (speedometers and so on) show that velocity could be perceived without reference to a 'clock,' but they do not tell us precisely how the neural system works. Some day it should be possible to draw a complete circuit diagram of the retina, and make a working electronic model of it, but this we cannot do with any confidence as yet for the human eye. A model has been suggested for the compound eye of beetles. This has been made and is now sometimes used in aircraft to detect drift due to wind blowing the machine off course. This movement detector was developed by biological evolution some hundred million years ago, discovered by applying electronic ideas, and then built with electronic components to be used for flight by man.

## The eye/head movement system

The neural system giving perception of movement by shift of images across the retina must be very different from the way movement is signalled by rotation of the eyes in the head. The eye movements are controlled by six extrinsic muscles for each eye; somehow, the fact that the eye is being moved is signalled to the brain and used to indicate the movement of external objects. That this really does happen is demonstrated with the cigarette experiment we have just described, for in that situation there is no systematic movement across the retina and yet the movement of the cigarette is seen when it is followed by the eyes (figure 7·2b).

The most obvious kind of signal would be feed-back from the muscles, so that when they stretch signals would be fed back to the brain indicating movement of the eyes, and so of objects followed by the eyes. This would be the engineer's solution, but is it Nature's? We find the answer when we look at what may seem a different question.

## Why does the world remain stable when we move our eyes?

The retinal images run across the receptors whenever we move our eyes, and yet we do not experience movement – the world does not spin round whenever we move our eyes. Why should this be?

We have seen that there are two neural systems for signalling movement, the *image/retina* and the *eye/head* systems – and it seems that during normal eye movements, these cancel each other out, to give stability to the visual world. The idea of cancellation to give stability was discussed by the physiologist who did most to unravel the spinal reflexes, Sir Charles Sherrington, and by

Helmholtz, but they had very different ideas as to how it comes about, and especially how what we have called the eye/head velocity system functions. Sherrington's theory is known as the *inflow theory* and Helmholtz's as the *outflow theory* (figure 7·3). Sherrington thought that signals from the eye muscles are fed back into the brain when the eye moves to cancel the movement signals from the retina. This idea is familiar to engineers as feed-back, but neural signals from the eye muscles would take rather a long time to arrive, and we would expect a sickening jolt just after we move our eyes, before the inflow signals reach the brain to cancel the retinal movement signals. Helmholtz had a very different idea. He thought that the retinal movement signals are cancelled *not* by signals from the muscles, but by central signals from the brain commanding the eyes to move.

The issue can be decided by very simple experiments, which the reader can try himself. Try pushing an eye gently with the finger, while the other is closed by holding a hand over it. When the eye is rotated passively in this way, the world will be seen to swing round, in the opposite direction to the movement of the eye. Evidently stability does not hold for *passive* eye movements, though it does for the normal *voluntary* movements. Since the world swings round *against* the direction of the passive eye movements, it is evident that the image/retina system still works; it is the eye/head system which is not operating. We may well ask: why should the eye/head system work only for voluntary and not for passive eye movements? Sherrington thought that it works by sending down signals from stretch receptors in the eye muscles. Such stretch receptors are well known, and serve to give feed-back signals from the muscles which move the limbs. But it looks as though the eye/head system does not work this way, for the stretch receptors should surely provide some signals during passive movements of the eyes.

We may stop all retinal movement signals and see what happens during passive movements of the eye. This is easily done by staring at a bright light (or a photographic flash) to get an after-image. This produces a local area of fatigue like a photograph stuck on

7·3 Why does the world remain stable when we move our eyes? The *inflow theory* suggests that the movement signals from the retina (image/retina system) are cancelled by (afferent) signals from the eye muscles. The *outflow theory* suggests that the retinal movement signals are cancelled by the (efferent) command signals to move the eyes, through an internal monitoring loop. The evidence favours the outflow theory.

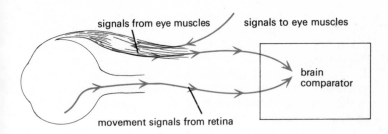

signals from eye muscles / signals to eye muscles

brain comparator

movement signals from retina

INFLOW THEORY

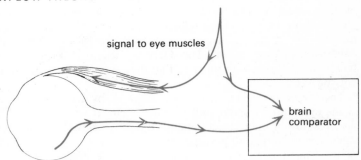

signal to eye muscles

brain comparator

OUTFLOW THEORY

the retina, and it will move precisely with the eye, and so cannot give any image/retina movement signals however the eye moves. If we observe the after-image in darkness (to avoid a background), it is found that if the eyes are pushed with the finger to move passively *the after-image does not move*. This is very strong evidence against the inflow theory, for stretch receptor activity should cause the after-image to shift with the eye, if it is normally responsible for cancelling the retinal movement signals.

If the eye is now moved voluntarily, you will find that *the after-image moves with the eye*. Wherever the eye is moved, the after-image will follow. Helmholtz explained this by supposing that it is not activity *from* the eye muscles which is involved, but *commands to move the eyes*. The outflow theory, as we have seen, holds that the command signals are monitored by an internal loop in the brain and cancelled against the retinal movement signals. When these are absent, as in the case of after-images viewed in darkness, the world swings round with the eyes because the command signals go uncancelled by the retina. Passive movements of the eye give no movement of after-images for neither system gives a movement signal.

In clinical cases where something has gone wrong with the eye muscles or their nerve supply, the world swings round for these patients when they try to move their eyes. Their world moves in the direction their eyes should have moved. This also occurs if the muscles are prevented from functioning, by *curare*, the South American arrow poison. The German scientist, Ernst Mach, bunged up his eyes with putty so that they could not move, and he got the same result.

The eye/head system, then, does not work by actual movement of the eyes, but by commands to move them. It works even when the eyes do not obey the command. It is surprising that command signals can give rise to perception of movement: we usually think of movement perception as coming from the eyes, not from a source deep in the brain controlling them.

Why should such a peculiar system have evolved? It is even more surprising, when we find that there are in fact stretch receptors in the eye muscles. An inflow or feed-back system would appear to be too slow: by the time a feed-back signal got back to the brain for cancelling against the retinal movement signal, it would be too late.

The cancelling signal could start at the same moment as the command, and so could oppose the retinal signal with no delay. Actually, the signal from the retina takes a little time to arrive (the 'retinal action time'), and so the command signal could arrive for cancelling too soon; but it is delayed to suit the retina, as we may see by studying carefully the movement of the after-image with voluntary eye movements. Whenever the eye is moved, the after-image takes a little time to catch up, and this is evidently the delay put into the monitored command signal so that it does not arrive before the signal from the retina. Can one imagine a more beautiful system?

## Illusions of movement

We may now look at some illusions of movement. Like other illusions they can be of practical importance, and they can throw light on normal processes.

### The case of the wandering light

The reader might like to try the following experiment. The apparatus is a single lighted cigarette placed on an ash-tray at the far end of a completely dark room. If the glowing end is observed for more than a few seconds, it will be found to wander around in a curious erratic manner, sometimes swooping in one direction, sometimes oscillating gently to and fro. Its movement may be paradoxical; it may appear to move and yet not to change its position. This perceptual paradox is important in understanding not only this phenomenon of the light that moves, but also the very basis of how movement is represented and coded in the nervous system.

This effect of the light that moves in the dark is known as the *autokinetic phenomenon*. It has received a great deal of discussion and experimental work. A dozen theories have been advanced to explain it, and it has even been used as an index of suggestibility and group interaction: for people tend to see it moving in the same direction that other people present claim to see it moving – though of course it is in fact stationary.

The theories to explain the effect are extraordinarily diverse. It has been suggested that small particles floating in the aqueous humour, in the front chamber of the eye, may drift about, and be dimly seen under these conditions. It is then supposed that the spot of light and not the particles *seems* to move, just as the moon may appear to scud through the sky on a night when the clouds are driven fast by the wind. This effect, known as 'induced movement,' will be discussed later. There is plenty of evidence however that it is not responsible for the autokinetic effect, for the movements occur in directions unrelated to the drift of the particles in the eye (when these are made more clearly visible with oblique lighting) and in any case they are not generally visible. A further theory – and one generally, though wrongly, held by ophthalmologists – is that the eyes cannot maintain their fixation accurately on a spot of light viewed in darkness, and that the drifting of the eyes causes the image of the spot of light to wander over the retina, causing the apparent movements of the light. This theory was all but disproved in 1928 by Guilford and Dallenbach, who photographed the eyes while the subjects observed the spot of light, and reported what movements they saw. The reported movements of the spot were compared with the photographic records of the eye movements, and no relation was found between the two. In addition, the eye movements under these conditions were extremely small. This experiment seems to have gone largely unnoticed.

All attempts but one to explain the wandering of the light in the dark suppose that *something* is moving – the particles in the aqueous humour, the eyes, or some sort of internal reference frame. This last suggestion formed an important part of the Gestalt psychologists' theory of perception. They attached great weight to the wandering-light effect. Koffka, in his celebrated *Gestalt Psychology* of 1935 says of it:

> These 'autokinetic movements', then, prove that no fixed retinal values belong to retinal points; they produce localisation within a framework, but do so no longer when the framework is lost. ... The autokinetic movements are the most impressive demonstration of the existence and functional effectiveness of the general spatial framework, but the operation of this framework pervades our whole experience.

This is not so clearly expressed as we might wish, but is the argument sound? I believe it contains an important fallacy.

What is true for the world of objects and their observation does not necessarily hold for errors of observation, or illusions. It is important to appreciate the difference. Any sense organ can give false information: pressure on the eye makes us see light in darkness; electrical stimulation of any sensory endings will produce the experience normally given by that sense. Similarly, if movement is represented in neural pathways, *we should expect to experience illusions of movement if these pathways are disturbed.* This is familiar with other, man-made, detectors of movement – the speedometer of a car may become stuck at a reading of, say, 50 km.p.h. and will indicate this velocity though the car is locked up in the garage.

The confusion, and it is a serious confusion, has, I believe, arisen through a failure to distinguish between the conditions necessary for *valid* estimates of the velocity of objects, and those holding for *invalid* estimates.

It is true that all real movement of objects in the world is relative, and we can only speak of, or measure, the movement of one object by reference to another object. Indeed this forms the basis of Einstein's Special Theory of Relativity. The point was indeed made clearly by Berkeley, in the seventeenth century, when he challenged a point in Newton's *Principia:*

> If every place is relative, then every motion is relative . . . Motion cannot be understood without a determination of its direction which in its turn cannot be understood except in relation to our or some other body. Up, Down, Right, Left, all directions and places are based on some relation and it is necessary to suppose another body distinct from the moving one . . . so that motion is relative in its nature. . . .
>
> Therefore, if we suppose that everything is annihilated except one globe, it would be impossible to imagine any movement of that globe.

But it has been assumed by writers on perception that if nothing is moving – not the eyes, particles in the eyes, nor anything else – it would be impossible to experience even *illusions* of movement, for example, of the spot of light in darkness. The wandering light has been taken to represent the same situation as Berkeley's globe when everything except it is annihilated, but it is very different.

The error lies in supposing that *false* estimates of movement, or

7·4 These 'clock histograms' show how a small dim light viewed in darkness appears to move after straining the eyes in four different directions for 30 seconds each time. The arrows show the direction of strain; the dark tinted areas show the direction of apparent movement for the next 30 seconds, while the light tinted areas show the movement during the following 30 seconds. The numbers give the duration in seconds of movement over two minutes after strain.

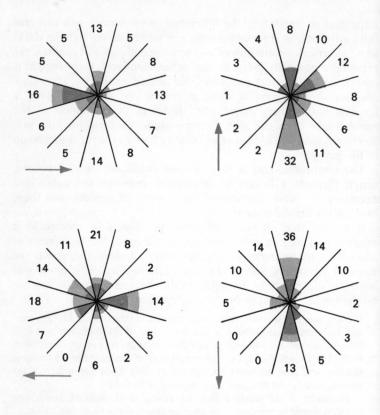

illusions of movement, require something moving relative to something else. But they can result simply from a disturbance, or a loss of calibration, of the measuring instrument – whether it be a speedometer or the eye. We may now seek for the kind of disturbance or loss of calibration of the visual system which is responsible for the wandering light. To do this we shall try to produce systematic movements of the spot of light, by deliberately upsetting the system.

If the eyes are held hard over for several seconds, in any direction, and then returned to their normal central position while the small dim light is viewed in darkness as before, the light will be seen to speed across in the direction in which the eyes were held – or possibly in the opposite direction but seldom in other planes. The movement may continue for several minutes if some of the eye muscles are considerably fatigued in this way (figure 7·4). Now fatigue of the eye muscles requires abnormal command signals to hold the eyes' fixation on the light, but these are the same as the signals which normally move the eyes when they follow a moving object. We thus see movement when the muscles are fatigued, although neither the eyes nor the image on the retinas are moving. The wandering illusory movements of the autokinetic effect seem to be due to the command signals maintaining fixation in spite of slight spontaneous fluctuations in the efficiency of the muscles, which tend to make the eyes wander. It is not the eyes moving, but the correcting signals applied to *prevent* them moving which cause the spot of light to wander in the dark.

We may now ask: if the correction signals move the spot of light in the dark, why do they not also cause instability under normal conditions? Why is the world generally stable? There is no certain answer to this question. It may be that in the presence of large fields of view the signals are ignored because the brain assumes that large objects are stable, unless there is clear evidence to the contrary. This is borne out by the effect of 'induced movement,' which we shall discuss, but first we should remember that sometimes the normal world does swing around.

### The case of the wandering world

The world swings round when we are fatigued or suffering from the less pleasant effects of alcohol. This was described by the Irish wit, Sheridan. Two friends led him to the front door of his house, in Berkeley Square, and left him. Looking back, they saw him still standing in the same position. 'Why don't you go in?' they shouted. 'I'm waiting until my door goes by again . . . then I'll jump through!' replied Sheridan. Just how this ties up with the wandering spot of light is not entirely clear. It may be that the eye movement command system is upset, or it may be that alcohol serves to reduce the significance of the external world, so that error signals which are normally disregarded are accepted. Just as we can become possessed by fantasies and irrational fears when tired or drunk, so also, perhaps, we become dominated by small errors in the nervous system which are generally rejected as insignificant. (If this is so, one might expect schizophrenics to suffer from instability of their visual world, but I know of no evidence for this.)

### The waterfall effect

We have seen that these movements of a light viewed in darkness are apparently due to small disturbances in the eye/head system. We might now expect to find similar illusions of movement due to disturbance of the image/retina system, and indeed we do. These illusions are not limited to movement of the whole field: various parts of the field may appear to move in different directions, and at different rates, the effects being bizarre and sometimes logically paradoxical. The most marked image/retina disturbance is known as the 'waterfall effect'.

The 'waterfall effect' was known to Aristotle. It is a dramatic example of illusory movement caused by adaptation of the image/retina system. It may be induced most easily by looking steadily, for about half a minute, at the central pivot of a rotating record player. If the turntable is then stopped suddenly it will seem, for

7·5 When this spiral is rotated, it appears to shrink or expand, depending on the direction of rotation. But when stopped, it continues to *appear* to shrink (or expand), in the *opposite direction*. This cannot be due to eye movement, since the apparent shrinkage or expansion occurs in all directions at once.
The effect is paradoxical – there is movement, but no change in position or size.

7·6 The waterfall effect. This is similar to apparent movement induced with the rotating spiral. After watching the moving stripes they appear to have a backwards-going velocity when stopped. This only occurs when the movement is observed with the eye held stationary, and *not following* the stripes. It must be due to adaptation of the image/retina system only.

several seconds, to be rotating backwards. The same effect is found after looking at moving water, for if the eyes are then directed to the bank, or any fixed object, it will seem to flow in the direction opposite to the flow of the water. The most dramatic effect is obtained from a rotating spiral (figure 7·5). This is seen to expand while rotating, and seems to contract as an after-effect when the spiral is stopped (or *vice versa* if the direction of rotation is reversed). This illusory contraction or expansion when the spiral is stopped cannot be due to eye movements, for the eyes can move only in one direction at a time while the effect is a radial contraction or expansion occurring in all directions from the centre at the same time. This fact alone shows that we must attribute the effect to the image/retina, rather than to the eye/head, movement system. It is also quite easy to show conclusively that it is *solely* due to upset of the image/retina system. This can be shown by following a moving belt of stripes with the eye, rapidly returning the eyes to the beginning of the belt of stripes when the end is reached, and following the movement again, several times. In this way continuous movement is experienced using the eye/head but not the image/retina system. When the belt is stopped, there is *no* after-effect, when the movement was seen by only the eye/head system (figure 7·6).

It remains a problem as to whether the adaptation takes place in the retina or in the brain. The retina seems rather too simple to be capable of such a complex after-effect, but it is very difficult to rule out retinal adaptation as a part-cause. One might think (and several psychologists who ought to have known better have thought) that the issue could be decided by looking at the moving stimulus object with one eye, while holding the other closed, and then observing whether the after-effect occurs when viewing a stationary object with the unstimulated eye. The answer is that it does occur, at about half strength. This does not, however, show conclusively that the adaptation took place in the brain, for it is possible that the stimulated eye goes on sending up a movement signal after it is shut and that this is, so to say, 'projected' into the

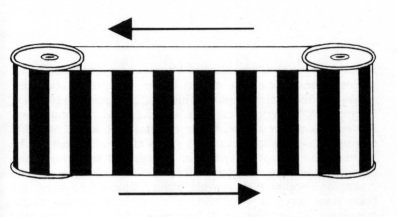

field of the unstimulated eye. This is perfectly possible, for it is difficult or impossible to say which eye is active: one tends to think that whichever eye is open is doing the seeing. There have been experiments to try to decide the issue.

We do not know precisely why the image/retina system is upset by continued stimulation by movement, because we do not know exactly how it works. We have already seen from the work of Hubel and Wiesel that movement is represented in separate neural channels, and that different channels indicate different directions of movement (figure 5·6). It is reasonable to assume that these channels can become adapted, or fatigued, with prolonged stimulation (as happens with almost all other neural channels) and that this unbalances the system, giving illusory movement in the opposite direction.

If the after-effect from the rotating spiral is examined carefully, two curious features will be noticed. The illusory movement may be paradoxical: it may expand or shrink, and yet be seen not to get bigger or smaller, but to *remain the same size and yet to grow*. This sounds impossible, and it *is* impossible for real objects, but we must always remember that what holds for real objects may not hold for perception once we suffer illusions. We can experience things which are logically impossible when we suffer illusions. In this case of the after-effect of movement of an expansion with no change in size, we may suppose that this comes about because *velocity* and *positions* are indicated by separate neural mechanisms, and only one of these – the velocity system – is upset by continued viewing of the rotating spiral. This is like a trial judge getting incompatible evidence from two witnesses and accepting both stories, at least for a time, before deciding that one is probably correct and dismissing the other as a pack of lies which can best be ignored. The perceptual system of the eye and brain has many channels, and many sources of information, and when for one reason or another they provide incompatible information, the brain must serve as judge. Sometimes different sources of incompatible information are, at least for a time, accepted together and then we experience a paradox – things that cannot possibly occur together. We should not be too surprised that illusions and hallucinations of drugs are sometimes impossible to describe.

After rather prolonged stimulation by the rotating spiral, the spiral's arms no longer look smooth curves, but seem made up of a series of short straight sections. These sections persist in the aftereffect, so that a circle viewed after watching the rotating spiral will appear to be a polygon. This curious effect suggests, perhaps, that direction of movement is represented by a rather small number of movement systems, arranged as vectors, and that adaptation shows up individual direction vectors. By counting the straight lines in the after-effect, one might hope to arrive at an estimate of the number of vectors involved, but it is curiously difficult to judge the number with confidence, even though the effect is in most people quite marked. A rough estimate would be about fifty, suggesting that *direction of movement* is given by about fifty vector systems. When these become unbalanced, by adaptation to sustained movement, we experience the waterfall phenomenon. This account is speculative, but it seems the best explanation.

A curious fact about the waterfall effect is that it occurs hardly at all if the moving field covers the entire retina and moves as a whole. It is *relative* movement in different parts of the retina which produces the effect. The reason for this is not fully understood, but it seems that the image/retina movement system is primarily concerned with relative movement. We are comparatively poor at detecting movements of objects when they are seen with no background, and thus no relative movement in different regions of the retina. It seems that it is this relative movement system which is adapted, and also that the adaptation is of a neural system indicating velocity directly and not as deduced from change of position/time. This fact – that stimulation of the whole retina gives very small or no after-effect – is fortunate, for it is largely because of this that car drivers seldom experience the effect, even when stopping suddenly after a lengthy run.

## Apparent movement

As we have seen, all the sensory systems can be fooled, but the most persistent fooling is by the cinema. Although in a cinema we are presented with a series of still pictures (twenty-four per second in sound films, and generally sixteen or eighteen in silent films) what we see is continuous action. This relies upon two rather distinct visual facts. The first is *persistence of vision*, and the second the so-called *phi phenomenon*.

Persistence of vision is simply the inability of the retina to follow and signal rapid fluctuations in brightness. If a light is switched on and off, at first slowly and then more frequently, one will see the light as flashing until at about thirty flashes per second it looks like a steady light. If the light is bright, the Critical Fusion Frequency (as it is called) is considerably higher, and may reach about fifty flashes per second. (This is a little unfortunate, for it is possible to be irritated by the flicker of the ends of fluorescent lamps, particularly when they fall on the edge of the retina.)

We have said that the separate pictures in the cinema are projected at twenty-four 'frames' per second, but this is well below the critical fusion rate, and so one may ask why we do not see a very flickering picture. In the early cinema this was indeed so (hence 'the flicks'), but modern projectors have a special shutter which shows each picture three times in rapid succession, so that although the number of pictures shown is only twenty-four in each second, the flicker rate is seventy-two flashes of light per second. This is above the critical fusion rate for all but the brightest parts of the picture when falling on the peripheral retina. Here some flicker may be seen.

Television gets over the problem of flicker rather differently. The picture is not presented as a whole, as in the cinema, but is built up in strips (known as an 'interlaced raster') which minimises flicker, though it *is* present and can be annoying, and even dangerous for people with a tendency to epilepsy who can be seriously affected by flicker. Indeed this is used for diagnostic purposes. It also presents a hazard in some rather unexpected circumstances, such as when driving by a row of trees whose shadows are cast upon the road by a low sun, or when landing a helicopter. The rotor blades of a helicopter produce a flickering light which can be most disturbing and dangerous.

Low-frequency flicker produces very odd effects on normal observers as well as on those with a tendency to epilepsy. At flash rates of about five–ten per second brilliant colours, and moving and stationary shapes, may be seen and can be extremely vivid. Their origin is obscure, but they probably arise from direct disturbance of the visual systems of the brain, the massive repeated bursts of retinal activity overloading the system. The patterns which are seen are so varied that it is difficult to deduce from their appearance anything about the kind of brain systems which have been disturbed. Stimulation by bright flashing lights can be an unpleasant experience, often leading to headache and nausea.

The other basic visual fact upon which the cinema depends is Apparent Movement, known as the 'phi phenomenon'. There is a vast literature of experimental studies on this effect. It is generally studied in the laboratory by using a very simple display – merely two lights which can be automatically switched so that just after one light has gone off the other comes on. What is seen – provided the distance between the lights and the time intervals between their flashes is about right – is a single light moving across from the position of the first light to the second. It was argued by the Gestalt psychologists that this apparent movement across the gap between the lights is due to an electrical charge or field in the brain sweeping across the visual projection area and filling in the gap. As it was thought that the phi phenomenon demonstrated such a process in the brain, it was studied intensively. Most authorities would now consider the Gestalt view of the matter mistaken. Consider once again the case of an image moving across the retina giving perception of movement as a result of the sequential stimulation of the receptors. If we leave out some receptors, between the two flashing lights or between the separate cinema pictures of a moving object, and we still see movement, do we have to suppose some special filling-in process? Is it not simply that the stimulus is adequate to actuate the retinal movement system provided the gaps in space or time are not too great? The situation is like that of a key and a lock. A key does not have to be *exactly* a certain shape to work the lock. There is always some degree of tolerance. Indeed, some tolerance is essential, for otherwise any slight change in the lock or the key would prevent it working. It is most likely that the image/retina system operates with stimuli reasonably like those provided by the normal movements of images, but that it will tolerate intermittent images provided the jumps in space or time are not too large. The phi phenomenon does tell us something about the image/retina system: namely, that it is reasonably tolerant in its demands – which makes the cinema and television economically possible.

## The relativity of movement

So far we have considered the basic mechanisms for perceiving movement – either by stimulation of the retina by moving images, or by the eye following objects. There is, however, far more to the perception of movement than this. Whenever there is movement, the brain always has to decide what is moving and what is stationary, with respect to some reference frame. Although, as we have

7·7 Induced movement. A spot of light is projected
on to a screen which is moved.
It is the stationary spot which is seen as moving.
This occurs when the moving part is larger, or more
likely to be stationary. (After Duncker.)

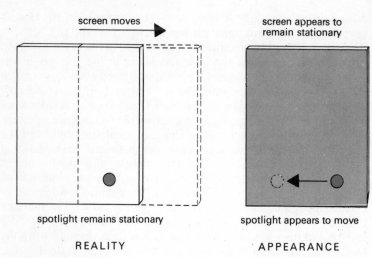

screen moves

screen appears to
remain stationary

spotlight remains stationary

spotlight appears to move

REALITY

APPEARANCE

seen, it is fallacious to suppose that illusory movement necessarily
involves any actual movement, it remains true that all real movement is relative, and a decision is always required. An obvious
example occurs whenever we change our position – by walking or
driving or flying. We generally know that the movement is due to
our own movements among the surrounding objects, and not due
to their movement, but it involves a decision. As we should expect,
sometimes the decision is made wrongly, and then we get errors
and illusions which can be particularly serious, because perception
of movement is of prime biological importance for survival. This
is as true in the case of man living in an advanced civilisation as
ever it was in the primitive state. Errors of movement perception
in flying or driving certainly cannot be ignored.

Most perceptual research has been undertaken with the observer
stationary – often looking into a box containing apparatus giving
him flashing lights, or pictures of various kinds. But real-life
perception occurs during free movement of the observer, in a
world where some of the surrounding objects are also in motion.

There are severe technical problems in investigating the real-life situation, but the attempt is well worth while, even though it does involve comparatively elaborate apparatus. The results can be important, not only for flying and driving, but also for space flight. It is still a real question just how far a human observer can be trusted to make decisions making a moon landing, when his entire previous visual experience has been limited to terrestrial conditions. In the unfamiliar surroundings of space, objects may be lit in strange ways, when perception of size and distance are upset. As we shall see, perception of size, distance and velocity are not separate but are related in a very complicated manner so that errors in any one can cause surprising errors in the others.

As we have seen, there is always a decision involved as to just what is moving. If the observer is walking, or running, there is generally not much of a problem, for he has a lot of information from his limbs, informing him of his movement in relation to the ground. But when he is carried along in a car or an aircraft the situation is very different. When he has his feet off the ground, his only source of information is through the eyes; except during acceleration or deceleration when the balance organs of the middle ear give some, though often misleading, information.

The phenomenon known as *induced movement* was very thoroughly investigated by a Gestalt psychologist, K. Duncker. He devised several elegant demonstrations which show that when there is movement known only by vision, we tend to accept that it is the largest objects which are stationary, the smaller objects moving. A striking demonstration is given by arranging a spot of light in a frame or background. If the frame (e.g. a cardboard screen, figure 7·7) is moved, what is seen is not the frame moving but the spot of light moving inside it, though in fact this is stationary. It should be noted that there actually is information available to the eye, for it is the image of the frame and not the spot which moves on the retina, but this information is not always sufficient to decide the issue. (This is relevant to the question of why the world is not always unstable, like the wandering light, discussed above.)

It seems clear that since it is generally rather small objects which move, the brain takes the best bet and tends to accept that movement is of smaller rather than larger objects when the issue can be in doubt. (The effect can be disturbing when driving a car – is it my hand-brake that is off, or is it that idiot over there running backwards?)

### Apparent movement and distance

When we observe the moon or stars while travelling in a car, we see them apparently moving along with us rather slowly. At fifty km. per hour, the moon may seem to move at ten–twenty km. per hour. We see it as moving more slowly than us, but keeping up, never falling behind. This is a curious effect.

The moon is so distant that we can regard it as being at infinity. As the car moves along, the angle to the moon remains virtually unchanged – it does not change its position although we are moving along under it. But perceptually it lies at a distance of only a few hundred metres. We know this from its apparent size. It subtends an angle of $\frac{1}{2}°$, but looks the size of an object subtending this angle placed a few hundred metres away. Now consider this comparison object a few hundred metres away, looking the same size as the moon. If we drive past *it* we rapidly leave it behind. But the moon does not get left behind, because it is in fact so distant, and the only way the perceptual system can reconcile these facts is to interpret them as an object moving with the car. The apparent velocity of the moon is determined by its apparent distance. (If the moon is observed through prisms to converge the eyes so that it appears at a different distance, it seems to move at a different speed.)

A related effect is observed with stereoscopic projection of lantern slides. If a scene is projected in stereo depth, using crossed polaroids, it seems to rotate – to follow the observer as he moves. Thus a picture in 3-D of a corridor swings round so that the apparent front moves with the observer, the corridor seemingly aimed at him. The effect is disturbing, and can lead to nausea. If the convergence of the eyes is increased, the entire scene, front and back, shifts across the screen whenever the observer moves. The effect is directly related to convergence and disparity, but it is not understood in all details, and would seem to repay research.

Stereo projection is particularly interesting in this connection because the objects observed in fact lie flat on the screen, although they are seen in depth, and so we have the situation of observer-movement with no motion parallax. Normally, when we move sideways, say to the right, nearer objects move to the left. Geometric-ally the world swings round the point of fixation of the eyes, against our movement. But when we observe pictures in stereo depth, the exact opposite happens; they appear to rotate *with* the observer's movement, the point of rotation being determined by the convergence of the eyes. This is set not at the will of the observer, but by the separation of the stereo pairs on the screen. (Given a stereo projector, these effects are well worth seeing.)

When the observer is carried along with his feet off the ground, he has to rely on vision to know that he is moving, and to judge his speed. In an aircraft there is little or no sensation of movement when flying high, and at landing and take-off it is a toss-up whether we see ourselves moving, or the ground rushing up to meet us. Illusions and errors in this situation are frequent and dramatic. So much so that pilots have to learn to dispense very largely with their normal perception, and to rely on instruments.

The situation is similar to that of induced movement. We make the best bet on very little evidence. The main evidence under normal conditions is systematic movement right across the retina, par-ticularly at the periphery. If, for example, a rotating spiral, like figure 7·5, is filmed and projected very large on a cinema screen, we seem to be moving towards, or away, from it – rather than seeing it expanding or contracting as when it fills but part of the eye. After all, it is not often that the whole of the retina receives systematic movement except when the cause is the eye moving. This is then the best bet. Hence the effectiveness of cinerama.

8·1 Thomas Young (1773–1829), after Lawrence. He was the founder with Helmholtz, of modern studies of colour vision. A universal genius, Young made important contributions to science and also to Egyptology, helping to translate the Rosetta Stone.

# 8 Seeing colour

The study of colour vision is an off-shoot from the main study of visual perception. It is almost certain that no mammals up to the Primates possess colour vision – if some do it is extremely rudimentary. What makes this so strange is that many lower animals do possess excellent colour vision: it is highly developed in birds, fish, reptiles and insects such as bees and dragon-flies. We attach such importance to our perception of colour – it is central to visual aesthetics and profoundly affects our emotional state – that it is difficult to imagine the grey world of other mammals, including our pet cats and dogs.

The history of the investigation of colour vision is remarkable for its acrimony. The problems have aroused more passion than passion itself. There is an extraordinary variety of theories, which never quite die; but when all is said, it is most likely that the first of all the theories is essentially correct.

The study of colour vision starts with Newton's great work, *The Opticks*. A word on this book is appropriate, as it is perhaps the scientific book of its period most worth reading today. *The Opticks* was written in Trinity College, Cambridge, in rooms which still exist and are still lived in. The classical experiments were conducted in these rooms – as also indeed were Newton's less successful experiments on the transformation of common metals into gold. In February 1692, his experiments on light were completed, and his book almost written, when the manuscript and all his notes were lost through a candle setting fire to them while he was in chapel. Newton was described by his contemporaries as being – understandably – much upset. He did not rewrite and publish the work until 1704 – it was his last book instead of his first – and it subsequently appeared in three more editions corrected by him (1717, 1721, and 1730), containing additions, notably to the celebrated 'Queries' which represent some of his most exciting speculations on the nature of the physical world.

Newton showed that white light is made up of all spectral colours, and with the development of the wave theory of light it became clear that each colour corresponds to a given frequency.

117

The essential problem for the eye, then, is how to get a different neural response for different frequencies. The problem is acute because the frequencies of radiation in the visible spectrum are so high – far higher than the nerves can follow directly. In fact the highest number of impulses a nerve can transmit is slightly under 1,000/second, while the frequency of light is a million million cycles/second. The problem is: How is frequency of light represented by the slow-acting nervous system?

This problem was tackled for the first time by Thomas Young (1773–1829) who suggested the theory, further developed by Helmholtz, which is still the best we have. Young's contribution was assessed by Clerk Maxwell, in the following words:

> It seems almost a truism to say that colour is a sensation; and yet Young, by honestly recognising this elementary truth, established the first consistent theory of colour. So far as I know, Thomas Young was the first who, starting from the well-known fact that there are three primary colours, sought for the explanation of this fact, not in the nature of light but in the constitution of man.

If there are receptors sensitive to every separable colour, there would have to be at least 200 kinds of receptor. But this is impossible – for the very good reason that we can see almost as well in coloured as in white light. The effective density of the receptors cannot therefore be reduced very much in monochromatic light, and so there cannot be more than a very few kinds of colour-responsive receptors. Young saw this clearly. In 1801 he wrote:

> Now, as it is almost impossible to conceive each sensitive point of the retina to contain an infinite number of particles, each capable of vibrating in perfect unison with every possible undulation, it becomes necessary to suppose the number limited, for instance, to the principal colours, red, yellow and blue . . .

Writing a little later, he stuck to the number of 'principal colours' as three; but changed them from red, yellow and blue, to red, green and violet.

We have now come to the hub of the problem: How can all the colours be represented by only a few kinds of receptor? Was Young right in supposing the number to be three? Can we discover the 'principal colours'?

The possibility that the full gamut may be given by only a few 'principal' colours is shown by a single and basic observation: colours can be mixed. This may seem obvious, but in fact the eye behaves very differently in this respect from the ear. Two sounds cannot be mixed to give a different pure third sound, but two colours give a third colour in which the constituents cannot be identified. Constituent sounds are heard as a chord, and can be separately identified, at any rate by musicians, but no training allows us to do the same for light.

We should be very clear at this point just what we mean by mixing colours. The painter mixes yellow and blue to produce green, but he is not mixing lights; he is mixing the total spectrum of colours *minus the colours absorbed by his pigments*. This is so confusing that we will forget about pigments, and consider only the light which is left after passing through a coloured filter, or produced by a prism or an interference grating.

Yellow is obtained by combining red with green light. Young suggested that yellow is always seen by effective red/green mixture, there being no separate type of receptor sensitive to yellow light, but rather two sets of receptors sensitive respectively to red and green the combined activity of which gives the sensation yellow.

In fact the fulcrum of controversies over colour theories is the perception of yellow. Is yellow seen by combined activity of red/green systems, or is it primary, as its simple perceptual quality might suggest? Although the simple appearance of yellow – it does not *look* like a mixture – has been raised against Young, this objection is invalid. The fact is that if a red and green light are mixed (e.g. by projecting these lights on a screen) we do see yellow, and the sensation is indistinguishable from that given by mono-chromatic light from the yellow region of the spectrum. It is certain that in this instance simplicity of sensation is no guide

8·2 Young's experiment on colour mixture. By mixing three lights (not pigments) widely spaced along the spectrum, Young showed that any spectral hue could be produced by adjusting the relative intensities suitably. He could also make white, but not black or non-spectral colours such as brown. He argued that the eye effectively mixes three colours, to which it is basically sensitive. This remains the key idea in explaining colour vision.

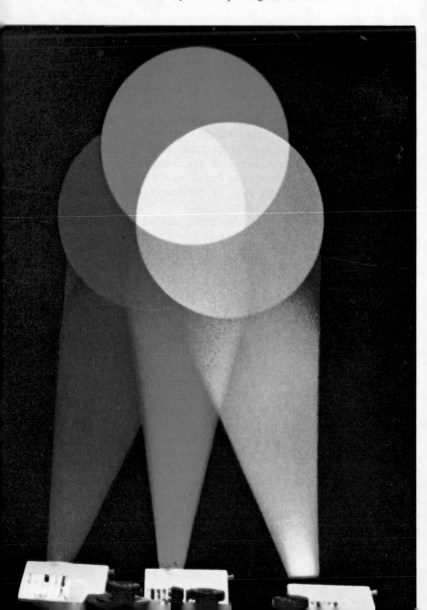

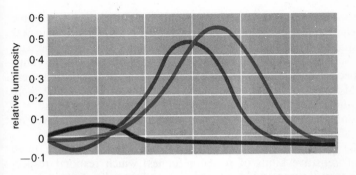

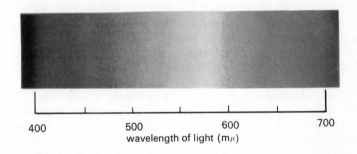

8·3 The fundamental colour response curves of the eye, according to W. D. Wright. These represent the supposed absorption curves of the three colour-sensitive pigments, all colours being seen by effective mixture of these.

to simplicity of the underlying neural basis of the sensation; and it seems that this is generally true for all sensations and perceptions.

Young chose three 'principal colours' for a very good reason. He found that he could produce any colour visible in the spectrum (and white) by mixture of three, but not less than three, lights set to appropriate intensities. He also found that the choice of suitable wavelengths is quite wide, and this is why it is so difficult to answer the question: what are the principal colours? If it were the case that only three particular colours would give by mixture the range of spectral hues, then we could say with some certainty that these would correspond to the basic colour systems of the eye, but there is no unique set of three wavelengths which will do the trick.

Young's demonstration is very beautiful. Figure 8·2 gives an idea of what it looks like.

The Young–Helmholtz theory is, then, that there are three colour-sensitive kinds of receptor (cones) which respond respectively to red, green and blue (or violet), and that all colours are seen by mixture of signals from the three systems. A great deal of work has gone into trying to isolate the basic response curves, and this has proved surprisingly difficult. The best established curves are shown in figure 8·3.

We may now look at a further graph, and one fundamental to the understanding of colour vision – the so-called hue-discrimination curve (figure 8·4). This compares wavelength of light with the smallest difference which produces a difference in hue. Now if we look at the earlier graph (figure 8·3) we see that hue should change very little as wavelength is varied at the ends of the spectrum, for the only change there is a gradual increase in the activity of the red or the blue systems, with no other system coming into play. We should see at the ends of the spectrum a change in brightness but not in colour. This is what happens. In the middle of the spectrum, on the other hand, we should expect dramatic changes in colour as the red system rapidly falls in sensitivity and the green rapidly rises – a small shift of wave-length should produce a large change in the relative activities of the red and green systems, giving a marked change of hue. We should thus expect hue discrimination to be exceptionally good around yellow – and this is indeed the case.

We shall pass over the later acrimonious debates on whether there are three, four or seven colour systems, and accept Young's notion that all colours are due to mixtures of three colours. But there is more to colour vision than that revealed by experiments with simple coloured patches. Recently a jolt has been given to the more complacent by the American inventive genius Edwin Land. Apart from inventing Polaroid, when a research student, and later developing the Land camera, he has shown with elegant demonstrations that what is true for colour mixture of simple patches of light is not the whole story of the perception of colour. Odd things happen when the patches are more complicated, and represent objects. What Land has recently shown has been known in general for many years, but to him belongs the credit of emphasising the additions to colour experience brought about by the more complicated situations of photographs and real objects. Indeed his work serves to remind us of the dangers of losing phenomena through simplifying situations in order to get neat experiments.

What Land did was to repeat Young's colour mixture experiment, but using not simple patches of light but photographic transparencies. Now, we may think of all projection colour photography as essentially Young's experiment put to work, for colour films provide physically only three colours. Land simplified it to two, and found that a surprising wealth of colour is given by only two actual colours. The technique is to take photographic negatives of the same scene, each through different colour filters. The negatives are converted into positive transparencies, and projected through their original filters, to give superimposed pictures on the screen. Quite good results are obtained simply with a red filter for one projector and no filter for the other. Now on Young's experiment, we would expect nothing but pink of varying saturation (amount of added white), but instead we get green and other colours not physically present. This kind of result might, however, have been anticipated from two well known facts. First, the early colour films used only two colours, but it was not realised how good they could be. Secondly, as we have seen, although Young found that the spectral hues and white could be

8·4 Hue discrimination curve. This shows how the smallest difference in wavelength ($\Delta\lambda$) varies with the wavelength of light ($\lambda$). It should be smallest (best colour discrimination) where the fundamental response curves (figure 8·3) have their steepest slopes. Roughly, this is true.

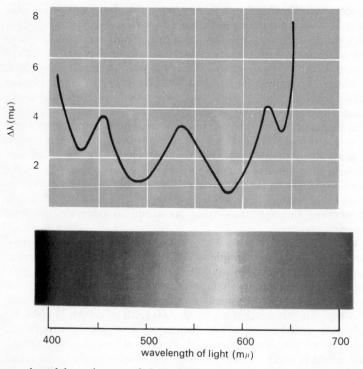

produced by mixture of three lights, it is *not* possible to produce *any* colour that can be seen. For example, brown cannot be produced, and neither can the metallic colours, such as silver and gold So there is something odd about three colours, let alone two.

Consider an ordinary kodachrome colour transparency projected on to a screen. This gives us all the colours we ever see, and yet it consists of only the three lights of Young's experiment. The colour film is no more than a complex spatial arrangement of three coloured filters, and yet this gives us brown and the other colours Young was unable to produce with his three colours. It seems that when the three lights are arranged in complex patterns, and especially when they represent objects, we see a greater wealth of colour than when the same lights are present as a simple pattern as in figure 8·2.

This means that any simple account of colour vision is doomed to failure: colour depends not only on the stimulus wavelengths and intensities, but also on whether the patterns are accepted as representing objects, and this involves high-level processes in the brain which are extremely difficult to investigate. Brown is a kind of super-saturated yellow (it can be produced by adapting the eye to the complementary colour to yellow, and then stimulating with yellow light) but normally it requires contrast, pattern, and preferably interpretation of areas of light as surfaces of objects before brown is seen, and yet in normal life brown is one of the most common colours. The eye tends to accept as white not a particular mixture of colours, but rather the general illumination whatever this may be. Thus we see a car's headlamps as white while on a country drive, but in town where there are bright white lights for comparison, they look quite yellow; and the same is true of candle or lamplight. This means that if the reference for what is taken as white is shifted, the position is complicated. Expectation, or previous knowledge, of the normal colour of the objects is important. It is probable that objects such as oranges and lemons take on a richer and more natural colour when they are recognised as such, but this is certainly not the whole story. Land was careful to use objects whose colours could not have been known to the observers – objects such as reels of plastic-covered wire, and materials having woven patterns in coloured wool. He still got his dramatic results.

Whatever the final assessment, and there is wide divergence of opinion, it is clear that Land's work brings out the complicated additions made by the brain to sensory information when sensations are organised into perceptions of objects. It is all too easy in thinking about vision to concentrate on the eye and forget the brain.

## Colour blindness

It is quite remarkable that even the common form of colour confusion – red confused with green – was not discovered before the late eighteenth century, when the chemist John Dalton found that he could not distinguish certain substances by their colours although other people could do so without difficulty. The reason is no doubt in part that we name objects by a variety of criteria. We call grass green, though we have no idea whether the sensation is the same for different people. Grass is a certain kind of plant found on lawns, and the sensation of colour which it gives we all call 'green,' but we identify grass by other characteristics than its colour – the form of the leaves, their density and so on – and if we do tend to confuse the colour there is generally sufficient additional evidence to identify it as grass. We know it is supposed to be green, and we call it green even when this may be doubtful.

In the case of a chemist identifying substances, however, there are occasions when it is only the colour of the substance in its bottle which he can use for identification, and then his ability to identify and name colours as such will be put to the test. Tests of colour vision all depend on isolating colour as the one identifying characteristic, and then it is easy to show whether an individual has normal ability to distinguish between colours, or whether he sees as a single colour what to other people appear different.

The most common colour confusion is between red and green, as we have said, but there are many other kinds of confusion. Red/green confusion is surprisingly common. Nearly ten per cent of men are markedly deficient, though it is extremely rare in women. Less common is green/blue confusion. Colour blindness is classified into three main types, based on the supposed three receptor systems. They used to be called simply Red-, Green- or Blue-Blindness, but the colour names are now avoided. Some people are completely lacking in one of the three kinds of cone systems – they are now called *protanopes*, *deuteranopes* and *tritanopes* (after the first, second and third colour-sensitive systems) but this does not clarify the situation very much. These people require only two coloured lights to match all the spectral colours *they* can see. Thus Young's colour mixture result applies only to most people – not to extreme cases of colour blindness. It is more common to find not a complete absence of a colour system, but rather a reduced sensitivity to some colours. These are classed as *protanopia, deuteranopia* and *tritanopia*. The last, tritanopia, is extremely rare. People with these deficiencies are described as having *anomalous colour vision*. This means that although they require three-coloured lights to make their spectral colours, they use different proportions from the normal.

The proportions of red and green light required to match a monochromatic yellow is the most important measure of colour anomaly. It was discovered (by Lord Rayleigh, in 1881) that people who confuse red with green, either require a greater intensity of red, or of green, to match yellow. Special instruments are made for testing colour vision, which provide a monochromatic field placed close to a red-plus-green mixture field. The relative intensities of the red and green in the mixture can be varied until the mixture gives the same colour to the observer as the monochromatic yellow. The proportions are read off a scale, which indicates the degree of protanopia or deuteranopia. The instrument is called an anomaloscope.

Yellow seems such a pure colour that it has often been thought that there must be a special yellow set of receptors. But it can be shown quite simply, with an anomaloscope, that yellow is in fact always seen by effective mixture of red and green.

An observer adjusts an anomaloscope so that he sees an identical yellow in the mixture and monochromatic fields. He then looks into a bright red light, to adapt the eye to red. While the retina is adapted to red, he looks back into the anomaloscope, and is asked to judge whether the two fields still look the same colour. *He will see both fields as green*, and they will be the same green. The match is *not* upset by the adaptation to red, and so he will not require a different proportion of red and green light in the mixture

8·5 Is there a special 'yellow' receptor? This experiment gives the answer. It uses an *anomaloscope* – an instrument giving a red + green mixture field (appearing yellow), next to a monochromatic yellow field appearing identical. Adaptation to a red or a green light does not produce a breakdown of the match between these two fields; from which it follows that there cannot be a separate mechanism for seeing yellow – it is always seen by the combined activity of the red and green receptor systems.

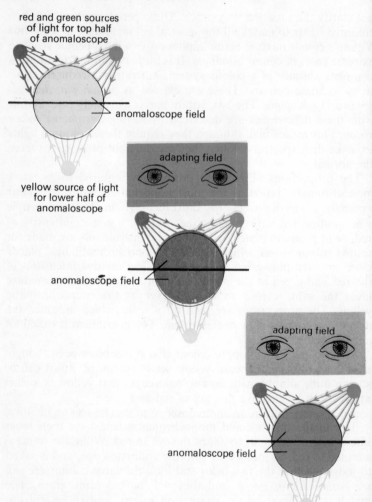

red and green sources
of light for top half
of anomaloscope

anomaloscope field

adapting field

yellow source of light
for lower half of
anomaloscope

anomaloscope field

adapting field

anomaloscope field

field to match the monochromatic yellow. It would therefore be impossible to tell from the setting of the anomaloscope that he has been adapted to red, though what he sees is quite different when adapted – a vivid green instead of yellow. The same is true for adaptation to green light – both fields will look *the same* red. The match still holds (figure 8·5).

But if there was a separate yellow receptor this could not happen. A separate yellow receptor would allow the monochromatic field to be seen as yellow in spite of adaptation to red or to green which must change the mixture field. A simple receptor could not get pushed along the spectrum scale by adaptation. But yellow seen by mixture of red and green receptor systems must be shifted if the sensitivity of the red or the green systems is affected by the adapting light. Thus there cannot be a different system operating for the two fields, or they would not be identically affected by adaptation to a coloured light. There is therefore no special yellow receptor.

The experiment may be repeated for other colours, with a similar result, showing that no colour has a special system. The same result is also obtained for anomalous observers: their initial setting is different, but it also remains unaffected by adaptation.

Now we come to a curious conclusion. If the anomaloscope cannot differentiate between the normal eye with and without colour adaptation, it follows that anomaly cannot be like colour adaptation. But this is exactly what colour anomaly *is generally supposed to be like*: namely a reduction in the sensitivity of one or more colour systems of the retina, through partial loss of a photo-pigment. This must be wrong. The reason for anomaly is not clear; there may be many causes, but it is certainly not due to a straight-forward shortage of photopigment, or the anomaloscope would not work. Some kinds of anomaly may be due not to reduced sensitivity of colour response systems, as in colour adaptation, but to spectral shift of response curves. Others might be due to neural 'short circuiting' of receptor systems so that two signal as though they were a single system.

9·1 René Descartes (1596–1650), perhaps the most influential of modern philosophers. It is now difficult to escape from his duality of mind and matter, which permeates all modern thought in psychology. He clearly described perceptual size and shape constancy, long before they were studied experimentally.

# 9 Illusions

Perception can go wrong in many ways. Most dramatic – an entire world may be created and mistaken for reality. This can happen in drug-induced states, or in mental disease. In addition to hallucinations, where experience departs altogether from reality, normal people may perceive surrounding objects in a distorted way. In this chapter we will pass rapidly over hallucinations, but spend some time on distortions giving rise to illusions of various kinds.

## Hallucinations and dreams

Hallucinations are similar to dreams. They may be visual or auditory, or may involve any of the other senses such as smell or touch. They may even combine several senses at once, when the impression of reality may be overwhelming. Hallucinations can be socially determined, and there are cases of many people 'witnessing' together events which never occurred.

There are two ways of regarding hallucinations, and these two ways go deep into the history of thought. Dreams and hallucinations have always excited wonder, and sometimes more, for they have affected human action, and sometimes brought about bizarre and terrible results.

To the mystic, dreams and hallucinations are insights into another world of reality and truth. Some recent thinkers regard the brain as a hindrance to understanding – a filter between us and a supraphysical reality, which allows us to see this reality clearly only when its normal function is disturbed by drugs or disease. To the more down-to-earth, however, including the empiricist philosophers, the brain is to be trusted only in health and hallucinations although interesting, and perhaps suggestive, are no more than aberrant outputs of the brain, to be mistrusted and feared. Aldous Huxley, in his *Doors of Perception*, represents and describes most vividly the viewpoint of the mystic, but the majority of neurologists and philosophers hold that truth is to be found only through the physical senses, while a disturbed brain is unreliable and not to be trusted as the purveyor of the truth.

To empiricists, hallucinations and dreams show the spontaneous activity of the nervous system when it goes unchecked by sensory information. A full-blown hallucination occurs when the spontaneous activity runs out of bounds.

The brain surgeon Wilder Penfield produces hallucinations when he stimulates regions of the brain with weak electric currents, and brain tumours may give persistent visual or auditory images, while the 'aura' preceding epileptic seizures may also be associated with hallucinations of various kinds. In these cases the perceptual system is moved to activity not by the normal signals from the sensory receptors, but by more central stimulation. It seems that the brain is always spontaneously active, and that the activity is normally under the control of sensory signals. When these are cut off (as in isolation chambers) the brain activity can run wild and instead of perception of the world we become dominated by hallucinations which may be terrifying and dangerous, or merely irritating or amusing.

There are many so-called hallucinogenic drugs which produce vivid and fantastic imagery, often associated with extreme emotional states. It is a matter of the greatest interest just why the brain is so affected by even minute concentrations of certain substances. Rather similar vivid imagery can occur in half-waking states (hypnogic imagery) when the experience can be like looking at a technicolour film, with the most vivid scenes apparently passing before the eyes although they are shut.

Hallucinations have also been found to occur when people are isolated in solitary confinement in prison, or experimentally in isolation chambers in which the light is kept subdued or diffused with special goggles, and nothing happens for hours or days on end. It seems that in the absence of sensory stimulation the brain can run wild and produce fantasies which may dominate. It is possible that this is part of what happens in schizophrenia, when the outside world makes little contact with the individual so that he is effectively isolated. These effects of isolation are interesting not only from the clinical point of view: they may present some hazard in normal life. Men may be effectively isolated for hours with very little to do in industrial situations, where control is taken from the operator by automatic machines which need only to be attended to in rare cases of emergency, and in space travel men could be isolated for long periods. This hazard is indeed a reason for sending more than one man into space.

In the author's opinion, there is no evidence for the mystic's attitude to hallucinations, for although the experiences may be extremely vivid they probably never convey information whose validity can be tested. But uncontrolled brain activity may indicate something of hidden motives and fears and so be revealing.

## Figures which disturb

There are some figures which are extremely disturbing to look at. These can be quite simple, generally consisting of repeated lines. The series of rays as in figure 9·2 or parallel lines as in figure 9·3 have been studied recently by D. M. McKay, who suggests that the visual system is upset by the redundancy of such patterns. The point is that given a small part of this figure, the rest can be specified by simply saying 'the rest is like what is given.' McKay suggests that the visual system normally uses the redundancy of objects to save itself work in analysing information. The ray figure is such an extreme case of a redundant figure that the system is upset by it. It is not entirely clear why this should happen, and one can think of other figures apparently just as redundant which do not upset the system, but it is an interesting idea and well worth following up. The ray figure has a curious after-effect; when looked at for a few seconds, wavy lines appear. These are seen for a time when the gaze is transferred to a homogeneous field such as a plain wall. It is a moot point whether the ray pattern produces these effects because of small eye movements shifting the repeated lines upon the retina, and so sending massive signals from the 'on' and 'off' receptors. If this is the explanation, the effect may be similar to the disturbance of flickering light. However this may be, the

9·2 Ray figure studied by McKay. Is it the redundancy of the figure which disturbs the brain? Or do the closely spaced lines stimulate the image/retina movement system, with each small movement of the eyes? If a blank wall is looked at after looking at this figure, there will be an after-effect like grains of rice in movement. This also occurs after watching movement, in the waterfall effect. The patterns of curved lines could be moiré patterns from after-images.

9·4 The Muller–Lyer, or *arrow illusion*. The figure with the outgoing fins looks longer than the figure with the ingoing fins. Why?

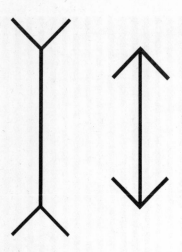

visual system certainly is disturbed, and this effect should be considered where repeated patterns are used in architecture.

## Visual distortions

Some simple figures are seen distorted. These distortions can be quite large. Part of a figure may appear twenty per cent too long, or too short; a straight line may be bent into a curve, so that it is difficult to believe it is really straight. Virtually all of us perceive these distortions, and in the same directions for each figure. It is believed that they occur also in animals. This is shown by training an animal to select, say, the longer of two lines. It will then select a line looking longer to us by virtue of an illusion when in fact it is the same length as a comparison line. This has been found for pigeons and for fish. All this suggests that there is something basic about these illusions. They are worthy of investigation.

Many theories have been put forward, but most can be easily

9·5 The Ponzo, or *railway lines illusion*. The upper horizontal line looks the
longer. This same line continues to look longer in whichever orientation
the figure is viewed. (Try rotating the book.)  137

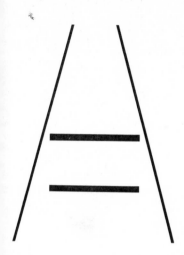

refuted experimentally or rejected as too vague to be helpful. We
will have a quick look at theories which can be safely rejected,
before trying to develop a more adequate theory. But first we should
experience some of the illusions themselves. Figures 9·4, 9·5 and 9·6
show many of the best known illusions. They are given with the
names of their discoverers, mainly nineteenth-century physicists and
psychologists working in Germany, but it may be convenient to
give some of them descriptive names.

The best-known is the *Muller-Lyer illusion*, shown in figure 9·4.
This is simply a pair of arrows whose shafts are of equal length, one
having outgoing and the other ingoing arrow-heads at each end.
The one with the outgoing heads looks considerably longer, though
it is in fact the same length, as may be checked with a ruler. We may
call this figure the *arrow* illusion (or if our theory, to be developed,
is right, the *corner* illusion).

The second example is the *Ponzo illusion* (figure 9·5). The cross
line in the narrower part of the space enclosed by the converging

9·6 Four classical illusion figures: **a** Hering – red lines bent;
**b** Orbison – square and circle distorted; **c** Poggendorf – red line
displaced; **d** Zöllner – red lines not parallel.

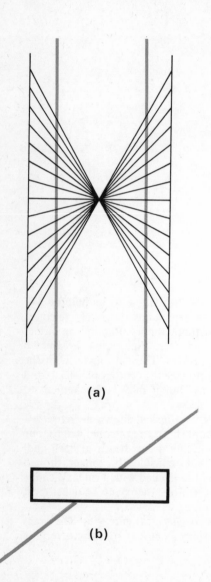

(a)

(b)

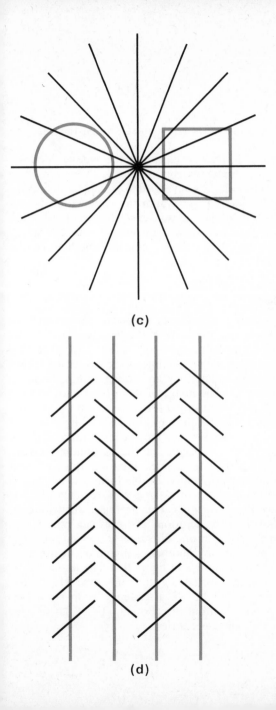

(c)

(d)

lines looks longer than the other cross line although they are the same length.

Figure 9·6 shows four further illusions: the Hering, Zöllner, Poggendorf and (two combined) Orbison figures.

Psychologists and physiologists have tried to explain the distortion illusions for the last hundred years and any explanation is still controversial. I believe however that we can safely reject most of the theories which have been proposed and develop a theory which accounts for the distortions and throws considerable light on the nature of perception.

### Theories we can reject

*1 The eye movement theory.* This theory supposes that the features giving the illusion make the eyes look in the 'wrong' place. In the arrow illusion, it is supposed that the eyes are drawn past the lines by the arrow-heads, which makes the lines look the wrong length or – an alternative theory – that they are drawn within the lines. But this cannot be correct. The image of the arrows may be fixed on the retina by optically stabilising it (or more simply by viewing, as an after-image, the figure with a bright flash of light from a photographic flash gun) and then eye movements cannot displace the image but the illusions still occur, and they are undiminished.

The eye movement theory is sometimes stated in rather different form, perhaps to avoid this difficulty. In this form it is not actual eye movements but the *tendency* to make eye movements which is supposed to produce the distortions. We can reject this with confidence, by the following consideration. The eyes can only move, or have a tendency to move, in one direction at a given time, but the distortions can occur in any number of directions at the same time. Consider the pair of arrows in figure 9·4. The first arrow is lengthened and the second shortened at the same time. How could this be due to an eye movement – or a tendency to an eye movement – which can occur in but one direction at a time? There is no evidence for the eye movement theories.

*2 The limited acuity theory.* Considering the arrow illusion – we should expect the figure with the outgoing fins to look too long, and the one with the ingoing fins to look too short if the acuity of the eye were so low that the corner could not be clearly seen. This may be demonstrated by placing a sheet of tracing paper over the figures, when a slight change of length might appear. The effect is however far too small to explain the Muller-Lyer illusion and it will not apply to many of the other illusions; so this is not a serious candidate, especially if we seek explanatory concepts to apply to most, preferably to all, the distortion illusions.

*3 Physiological 'confusion' theories.* Although we believe that physiological processes mediate all perception, thinking and experience, we can have specifically 'physiological' theories. They point to disturbance of components of mechanisms. Such disturbance might be caused by drugs, fatigue, or adaptation to intense or prolonged stimulation, as in the 'waterfall effect'. The distortion illusions are different from all these, for they occur in all normal people and immediately, without adaptation. Certain pattern features upset the perception of size and angle immediately: could it be that these features directly upset the orientation detectors (pages 68–71) discovered by Hubel and Wiesel? We should distinguish two kinds of theory along these lines:

(i) That orientation detectors exaggerate all acute angles and minimise all obtuse angles. Although this was effectively suggested by Helmholtz, and has been revived since, there is no convincing independent evidence. (Experiments where angles are named, in degrees, may be discounted.) It is inherently implausible that so basic a system would have large systematic errors.

(ii) That there are interactive effects between active orientation (or angle) detectors. It may again seem unlikely that the initial stages of pattern detection would be so 'ill-designed' that there would be serious interactions to generate errors, but a recent suggestion by Colin Blakemore has made this more plausible. Blakemore supposes that interactive effects capable of producing distortions may be *side-*

*effects* of the process known as lateral inhibition. If the distortions were an unfortunate consequence of such a process, then the apparent ill-design is understandable.

Lateral inhibition is interaction between regions such that regions of strong stimulation reduce the sensitivity of surrounding regions. This gives a kind of 'sharpening' effect for gradients of neural stimulation, which is economical, for it is generally peaks of stimulation which are important. Blakemore's suggestion is that converging or angled lines produce asymmetrical regions of lateral inhibition, which will shift the neurally signalled peaks of stimulation, to produce visual distortions. We may call this a 'physiological' theory because it invokes disturbance of functional units (nerve cells) rather than inappropriateness of what they are being called upon to do. In computer terminology this would be a 'hardware' not a 'software' error. Whether illusions should be regarded as 'physiological' in this sense, or 'cognitive' is a fundamental issue surprisingly difficult to decide – which makes illusions an interesting challenge.

Here are some difficulties which arise if one supposes that the illusions have such a 'physiological' origin:

(i) Shifts of position should be small, probably comparable to visual acuity, but the distortions are large.

(ii) It is the signalling of angles, rather than spatial positions or lengths, which are supposed to be disturbed. This raises the question: are these illusions essentially distortions of angle, or of positions or lengths? Several illusions (e.g. the Muller-Lyer, the Ponzo, the Zöllner and the Poggendorf) would appear to be changes in lengths, or parallel displacements of lines, without change of angle.

(iii) The shifts in position can be cumulative across many parallel lines (as in the Zöllner illusion) but there seems no reason why shifts should be cumulative from one border to the next by lateral inhibition.

(iv) The illusions still occur though different parts are presented to each eye, to be combined by central stereoscopic fusion, as by Julesz's experiment (pages 58–9). The lateral inhibition could not then be retinal but must occur after fusion of the two images, which is rather unlikely.

(v) The illusions occur even when drawn as widely separated dots, instead of the usual continuous lines. It is not clear whether or not lateral inhibition occurs across regions between dots where there is no physical stimulation. This is an urgent question for electro-physiological research.

(vi) Distortions occur in several figures having only right-angular or parallel lines, when lateral inhibition should be symmetrical. Examples: the horizontal/vertical illusion (vertical lines being longer than horizontal); the Zöllner figure drawn with right-angular lines and omitting the parallels when the 'herring bones' still appear displaced; the Muller-Lyer arrows with right-angular heads and the 'shafts' omitted, when the separations between the heads is still upset (figure 9·7); and Thiéry's figure (figure 9·8).

Although perhaps we cannot discount entirely the possibility of a 'physiological' (in computer terms, 'hardware') account of distortion illusions, we will go on to explore the alternative: that these illusions are due to inappropriate strategies, or 'software'. This will suppose that the errors arise not at the primary pattern recognition processes but rather at the cognitive level. This is most likely to occur when sensory patterns are interpreted in terms of sizes and distances of external objects: but we will first mention a very different cognitive theory.

*4 The empathy theory.* This theory was suggested by Theodor Lipps, and is based on an idea of the American psychologist, R. H. Woodworth. The idea is that the observer identifies himself with parts of the figure (or with say the pillars of a building) and that he becomes emotionally involved so that his vision is distorted rather as emotion may distort an intellectual judgment. In the arrow illusion, it would be argued that the outgoing arrow suggests, emotionally, expansion which one then sees.

It is true that a very thick column supporting a narrow cornice on a building looks clumsy; and perhaps one does imaginatively

9·1 Muller-Lyer arrow heads (*left*), drawn as right-angles and without shafts. Here there are only right-angles and parallel lines, and yet the illusion still occurs. This is difficult to explain on a 'lateral inhibition' theory; but this is still a perspective figure, and could set constancy size scaling to produce the distortion.

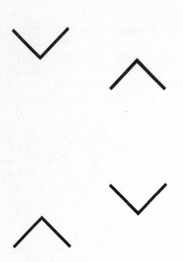

stand in the place of the column, much as Hercules took the load of the sky off the shoulders of Atlas before turning him to stone. The caryatids of Greek temples (figure 9·9) embody (quite literally) this idea in architecture. But although of immediate relevance to aesthetics, it can hardly be taken seriously as a theory of the illusions. The arrow figure (for example) gives distortion whatever one's mood, and continues to do so when any initial emotional response would surely have died through boredom. There may be perceptual effects of strong emotion, but the illusion figures would seem singularly devoid of emotional content – except indeed to those who try to explain them! More serious: the distortions are virtually the same for all observers though emotions are very different.

5 *The pregnance or 'good-figure' theory.* The idea of 'pregnance' is central to the German Gestalt writers on perception. The English meaning is similar to the use of the word in, for example, 'a

9·8 The *absence* of perspective generates distortion. The further edge would normally be shrunk by distance – to be compensated by constancy scaling. Here, evidently, the scaling is set by the assumption of depth, to produce distortion. (Hide the legs, and the distortion will disappear. It must be recognised as an object of familiar shape for distortion to occur; so this is not quite the same as the Muller-Lyer illusion, though it is related.)

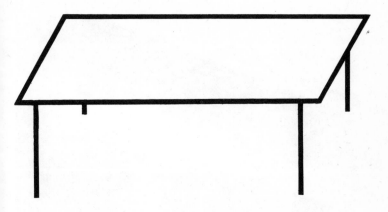

pregnant sentence.' A 'pregnant' figure is one expressing some characteristic although it is not all present. The illusions are supposed to be due to pregnance exaggerating the distance of features seeming to stand apart, and reducing the distance of the features which seem to belong together.

The status of the idea of pregnance is doubtful. Certainly random or systematic arrangements of dots do tend to be grouped in various ways, so that some belong to one figure while others are rejected or are organised into other patterns (figure 1·1) but there seems no tendency for the dots to change their position as a result of such grouping, and surely this would be an inevitable prediction of the pregnance theory of spatial distortion?

*6 The perspective theory*. This theory has a long history, into which we need not enter, but the central idea is that the illusion figures suggest depth by perspective, and that this suggestion of depth produces size changes.

9·9 Man enough for the job? Perhaps we identify ourselves with pillars, so that there is a right size in human terms for carrying the load. This is the basic idea of 'empathy', a key idea in aesthetics. It has also been suggested as a basis for visual illusions.

It certainly seems to be true that the illusion figures can be thought of as flat projections of typical three dimensional views. This is a most important point, for it leads to a fairly complete understanding of the illusions. Consider the three illusion figures we started with (figures 9·4, 5 and 6). Each of these can be fitted very naturally to typical views of objects lying in three dimensions. The illusion figures can be thought of as flat projections of three dimensional space – simple perspective drawings – and the following generalisation holds: *Those parts of the illusion figures which would represent distant objects are enlarged, and those parts representing near objects are diminished.*

This may be seen clearly in the arrow illusion. The arrow with the outgoing fins could represent the inside corner of a room (figure 9·10). The ingoing arrow-heads could represent an outside corner of a building (figure 9·11). The railway lines illusion fits converging perspective lines, placing the upper horizontal further away than the lower (figure 9·12).

It should be made clear at once, however, that although the illusion figures do seem to be typical flat projections of three dimensions, each one *could* always represent something quite different. The arrow figures could represent a steeplejack's view of a roof; the converging lines of the railway lines illusion *could* simply be a pair of converging lines, rather than parallel lines seen as converging because of distance. The illusion figures are typical perspective views, but in all cases they could be drawings of something quite different.

The traditional perspective theory simply states that these figures suggest depth, and that if this suggestion is followed the more distant features appear objectively larger. But why should suggestion of distance produce a change in apparent size? Further, why should suggestion of greater distance produce *increase* in size when distant objects are typically seen as *smaller* with increasing distance? The theory predicts not an increase, but a decrease in the size of features having greater distance indicated by perspective, but this is the wrong way round.

9·10 An inside corner. The edges of the ceiling and walls, and the floor and walls, form the same retinal image as the outgoing Muller–Lyer arrow illusion figures. (Note that the corner of the wall would be furthest away in the actual room.)

9·11 An outside corner. The line of the top and bottom of the building form the ingoing arrow illusion. (Note that the corner of the building would be nearest to the observer.)

9·12 The railway lines form the same retinal image as the Ponzo illusion. (Note that the actually equal white rectangles are changed in size as in the Ponzo line figure.)

### Towards an answer

Although the predictions of the perspective theory go the wrong way, this is far better than predictions which are quite unrelated to the facts. It does look as though there may be something important in the perspective idea. We will now try to develop a theory of the illusions which incorporates the perspective suggestion, but leads

9·13 Size constancy. The image of an object halves in size with each doubling    151
of the distance of the object. But it does not *appear* to shrink so much.
The brain compensates for the shrinkage of the image with distance, by a
process we call *constancy scaling*. (It is here that we find the secret
of the distortion illusions.)

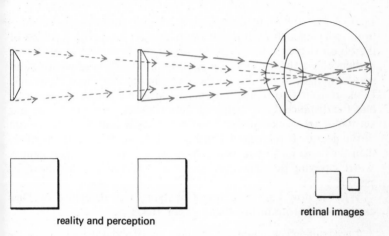

reality and perception

retinal images

to correct predictions, as well as linking the illusions to other perceptual phenomena. It is worth devoting some time to this, for it is by establishing connections between phenomena that we gain understanding. Illusions become no longer trivial effects of certain patterns, but rather tools for investigating basic processes involved in seeing the world.

There is a perceptual process which is quite capable of producing distortions – Size Constancy. This is the tendency for the perceptual system to compensate for changes in the retinal image with viewing distance. It is a remarkable and fascinating process which in certain conditions we can see operating in ourselves. It can go wrong; and when it does, instead of keeping the visual world relatively stable it may produce instability and distortion. This linking of perceptual constancy with the illusions is a rather new idea. We will describe experiments aimed at testing this after we have discussed constancy in more detail.

The image of an object doubles in size whenever its distance is halved. This is a simple fact from geometrical optics, and applies to a camera as it does to the eyes. Why it occurs should be clear from figure 9·13. Now what is odd, and it certainly requires some explanation, is the fact that although the image grows as the distance of the object decreases *it still looks almost the same size*; consider an audience at a theatre – the faces all look much the same size, and yet the images of the distant faces are far smaller than the nearer. Look at your two hands, one placed at arm's length the other at half the distance – they will look almost exactly the same size, and yet the image of the further hand will be only half the (linear) size of the nearer. If the nearer hand is brought to overlap the further, then they *will* look quite different in size. This little experiment is worth carrying out. The overlap defeats constancy – and shows its power.

What is now known as Size Constancy was described by Descartes, who wrote in his *Dioptrics*, of 1637:

> I need not, in conclusion, say anything special about the way we see the size and shape of objects; it is completely determined by the way we see the distance and position of their parts. Thus, their size is judged according to our knowledge or opinion as to their distance, in conjunction with the size of the images that they impress on the back of the eye. It is not the absolute size of the images that counts. Clearly they are a hundred times bigger when the objects are very close to us than when they are ten times farther away; but they do not make us see the objects a hundred times bigger [the area, not the linear size]; on the contrary, they seem almost the same size, at any rate so long as we are not deceived by (too great) a distance.

We have here as clear a statement of size constancy as any made later by psychologists. Descartes goes on to describe what is now called Shape Constancy:

> Again, our judgments of shape clearly come from our knowledge, or opinion, as to the position of the various parts of the objects, and not in accordance with the pictures in the eye; for these pictures normally contain ovals and diamonds when they cause us to see circles and squares.

The ability of the perceptual system to compensate for changing distance has been very fully investigated, notably by the English psychologist Robert Thouless in the 1930's. Thouless measured the amount of constancy under various conditions, and for different types of people. He used very simple apparatus – nothing more elaborate than rulers and pieces of cardboard. For measuring size constancy he placed a square of cardboard at a given distance from the observer, and a series of different sized squares at a nearer position. The subject chose a square at this second distance appearing the same size as the further. From the actual sizes, the amount of size constancy could easily be calculated. Thouless found that his subjects generally chose a size of square almost the same as the actual size of the distant square, although its image was smaller than the image of the near square. Constancy was generally almost perfect for fairly near objects, though it broke down for distant objects, which do look small, like toys. Constancy did not hold when there were few depth cues available. Highly critical subjects showed less constancy, and this was also true for trained artists. As Descartes had implied 300 years before, there is a perceptual scaling system which makes objects placed at different distances appear 'almost equal in size, at least if we are not deceived in respect of their distance.' Thouless also measured shape constancy, and this he did by cutting out a series of cardboard 'lozenges' or ellipses of various eccentricity, which were selected by the subject to match a cardboard square or circle placed at an angle to the subject's line of sight – the comparison lozenge or ellipse being placed normal to the subject. Again it was found that constancy was nearly but not quite perfect, and again subjects differed quite a lot in their amount of constancy; highly critical people and trained artists again tending to show less constancy, while a few individuals could change their amount of constancy more or less at will in this experimental situation.

It is possible to see one's own constancy scaling at work. It takes only a moment, and is most striking.

First a good clear after-image is obtained, by looking steadily at a bright light (preferably a photographic flash); and then a wall or screen is looked at. The after-image will lie on the screen and will take on the distance of the screen. The experiment is simply this: having got a good clear after-image, direct the eyes at a near screen, say a book or the palm of the hand, and then look at a distant wall of the room. It will be found that the after-image changes dramatically in size. It is smaller when seen as near, and much larger when seen as lying in the distance. In fact the after-image will very nearly double in size as the screen on which it lies doubles in distance. This inverse relation between size and distance is known as Emmert's Law.

The expansion of the after-image with increasing distance is due to the constancy scaling which normally compensates for the shrinking of the image with distance. Here the image does not shrink, being fixed on the retina, and so we see our own constancy scaling at work.

We may now return to the illusions. If the constancy scaling tending to compensate for distance were triggered by perspective depth features, then we should expect the observed distortions in the illusion figures. This is a very reasonable theory. It has the great merit that it does not postulate anything we do not already know. It puts together two well known phenomena; suggesting that the distortions are produced by constancy scaling when this is misapplied. Since the illusion figures are in fact flat, we can easily see that if the perspective features do set the constancy it must be inappropriate. The parts of the figures indicated as more distant would be expanded. This is what happens.

It is one thing to have a theory and quite another to prove it. In fact there is a great difficulty in this theory as we have so far described it. The illusion figures generally look flat. We must explain, why the illusion figures look flat in spite of their perspective features, and, how constancy can be set although the figures look flat, when Emmert's Law shows that constancy functions according to apparent distance. It is, I believe, this difficulty which has prevented serious consideration of the theory, until recently. We must now see whether it can be surmounted.

The first difficulty is not too great. When we look at the figures, we see not only the figures but also the paper on which they are drawn. The figures look flat because they lie on a flat surface. What happens if we keep the figures but remove the surface? This is easily done, by making wire models of the figures and painting them with luminous paint to glow in the dark. If the luminous illusion figures are observed in darkness, looking at them with one eye to avoid stereoscopic information of their true depth, or lack of it, we find that they *look three dimensional*. The arrow figure, for instance, no longer looks flat: it looks like a corner. The arrow with the outgoing fins looks like an inside corner, and the arrow with the ingoing fins like an outside corner, as indicated by perspective, and they are indistinguishable from truly three-dimensional wire model corners. This observation provides the clue to why they normally look flat: the texture of the paper gives competing information to the perspective of the figures, preventing their appearance in depth. This is a matter of importance to the artist, for the texture of his paper or canvas will always compete with the texture and the other depth cues of his work, preventing it from being seen as three-dimensional. Remove the texture and remarkable depth is seen. This is why coloured photographic transparencies in a simple viewer can look more convincingly in depth than when projected on a screen, especially if the light is rather dim so that slight imperfections of the surface of the transparency are not revealed.

The second difficulty – that constancy follows apparent distance as revealed by Emmert's Law – is more difficult to attack, and it is held with great authority. Thus Ittleson, citing for support five distinguished psychologists who have worked on the problem, has this to say: 'Constancy, it is universally agreed, is dependent upon the proper estimation of distance.' Nevertheless, I will challenge this assumption as I believe it not only to be wrong but to have inhibited the development of an adequate theory of illusions.

Illusion figures generally appear flat, and it is true that constancy does follow apparent distance, as in Emmert's Law; but it does not follow that constancy is necessarily tied to apparent distance. There is no reason why it should not be triggered by depth cues even when these are countermanded by other cues, as happens when perspective or illusion figures are drawn on textured paper. If we could show that this does happen, then we have explained the illusions and also learned something new about constancy.

We should now look for independent evidence that it is misplaced constancy which gives the distortions. This becomes a technical and quite complicated matter, but here is some of the evidence.

1. We can put to use figures which are ambiguous in depth. These figures (for example the Necker cube, figure 1·4) give rise to alternative perceptions of depth and yet the retinal image – the input to the brain – remains constant. Now if we look carefully at a Necker cube, we find that although a face alternates with another in depth, *they do not change in size*. This immediately tells us that constancy is not evoked, or set, by the depth suggested by this figure drawn on paper. Now if we make a luminous cube (a wire model coated with luminous paint to glow in the dark so as to avoid the textured background of the paper), we get a quite different result. When our luminous cube reverses in depth, it *does* change shape. The face that appears further away, whichever it is, looks larger, though the two faces are in fact the same size. Thus we now see Emmert's Law applying to depth ambiguous figures. If we make a true three dimensional cube, we find that when this reverses we see a truncated pyramid instead of a cube, the apparently nearer face appearing smaller than the apparently more distant face: constancy is now working backwards, according to apparent and not true depth, and producing distortion when perceptual depth reverses. This may suggest that perception of depth is essential to constancy: but consider the following. Take a cube figure drawn on paper, but with a line added as in figure 9·14. This line, although in fact straight, appears bent at the corner of the cube figure. Now observe this line carefully when the cube reverses in (paradoxical) depth, and you will see that the line still appears bent the same way. Now this is quite different from what happens

9·14 The line drawn across the corner of the Necker cube appears slightly bent, though in fact it is straight. It appears bent the same way when the cube reverses in depth. It follows that the illusory bending is *not* the result of apparent depth. But if the cube is luminous, the line does bend with each change in orientation of the Necker cube.

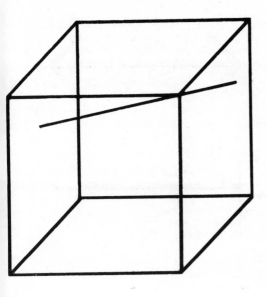

when a similar line is added to a *luminous* Necker cube, or a wire cube: then the line will still appear bent (by constancy) but the direction of bend changes as the cube changes in apparent depth.

The bend of the line across the cube figure with background is determined not by whether that corner looks ingoing or outgoing, but simply according to whether that corner would typically be an ingoing or outgoing corner. This is important, for it suggests that the illusory bend of the line is not due to constancy working according to apparent depth but directly according to the depth cues, though these are countermanded by the texture of the paper which makes the cube appear flat. If we place a line like this across a *luminous* cube, then the direction of the bend of the line changes as the cube apparently lies first in one apparent orientation then in the other – Emmert's Law takes over.

9·15 How to measure an illusion. The observer sees a single arrow figure and an adjustable comparison line, which is set to appear the same length as the distorted line. This gives a direct measure of the extent of the illusion. (Measurement is only possible, however, when the illusion is not logically paradoxical.) The figure shows a back view of the apparatus.

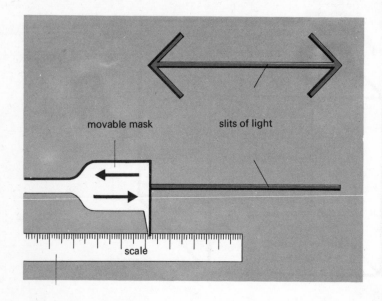

movable mask          slits of light

scale

2. It is possible to measure apparent depth, as given by perspective or other depth cues, with a technique giving an objective measure of the apparent depth. This technique (devised by the author) makes it possible to relate directly apparent depth to the illusions.

It is quite easy to measure the amount of an illusion of the kind we are considering here – distortions of size or shape. It can be done by showing a set of comparison lines, or shapes, and asking the observer to select the one most like the illusion figure as he sees it. Of course, it is essential to show the comparison line in such a way that *it* is not distorted! In practice it sometimes is better to arrange for the comparison line, or figure, to be continuously adjusted, either by the observer or the experimenter. A suitable apparatus is shown in figure 9·15.

Measuring apparent depth is more difficult. It may even seem to be impossible. But consider figure 9·16. The figure is presented

·16 How to measure subjective visual depth. The (flat) figure is back
illuminated, to avoid texture which gives it paradoxical depth. The light from
the figure is cross-polarised to one eye. An adjustable reference light is introduced
into the figure, by reflection from a half-silvered mirror. This is seen with
*both* eyes, and is set to the apparent distance of any selected parts of the
figure. Thus binocular vision is used to measure monocular depth.

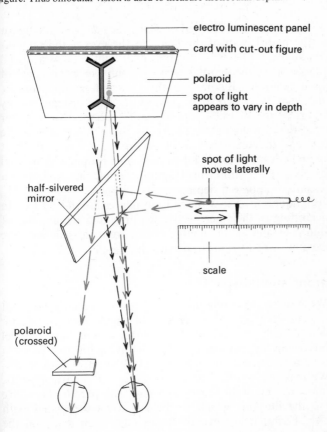

back-illuminated, to avoid texture, and it is viewed through a sheet
of polaroid. A second sheet of polaroid is placed over one eye,
crossed with the first so that no light from the figure reaches this
eye. Between the eyes and the figure, is a half-silvered mirror
through which the figure is seen but which also reflects one or
more small light sources mounted on an optical bench. These

appear to lie in the figure: indeed optically they *do* lie in the figure provided the path length of the lights to the eyes is the same as that of the figure to the eyes. But the small light sources are seen with *both* eyes while the figure is seen with only *one* eye because of the crossed polaroid. By moving the lights along their optical bench, they may be placed so as to lie at the same distance as any selected part of the figure. If the figure has perspective or other depth cues, then the lights are placed by the observer not at the true distance of the figure, but at the apparent distance of the part of the figure he is matching lights against. For people with normal binocular depth perception, this is quite a simple task and gives a good measure of apparent depth.

This technique shows that the illusion figures are indeed seen in depth, according to their perspective features, and the amount of the illusion is greater as the depth features are increased. We have thus related these distortions to perspective depth.

## Distortions and perspective

In the Western world rooms are nearly always rectangular; and many objects, such as boxes, have right-angled corners. Again, many things, such as roads and railways, present long parallel lines converging by perspective. People living in the Western world have a visual environment rich in perspective cues to distance. We may ask whether people living in other environments, where there are few right angles and few long parallel lines, are subject to the illusions which we believe to be associated with perspective. Fortunately, several studies have been made on the perception of people living in such environments, and measurements have been made of their susceptibility to some of the illusion figures.

The people who stand out as living in a non-perspective world are the Zulus. Their world has been described as a 'circular culture' – their huts are round, and have round doors; they do not plough their land in straight furrows but in curves; and few of

9·17 The circular culture of the Zulus. They experience few straight lines or corners and are not affected by the illusion figures to the same extent as people brought up in a 'rectangular' Western culture.

their possessions have corners or straight lines. They are thus ideal subjects for our purpose. It is found that they do experience the arrow illusion to a small extent, but they are hardly affected at all by the other illusion figures.

Studies of people living in dense forest have been made. Such people are interesting, in that they do not experience distant objects, because there are only small clearances in the forest. When they are taken out of their forest, and shown distant objects, they see these not as distant, but as small. People living in Western cultures experience a similar distortion when looking down from a height. From a high window objects look too small, though steeple-jacks and men who work on the scaffolding and girder structure of skyscrapers are reported to see objects below them without distortion. It seems that active touch is important in setting the visual scale of objects.

This point comes out in the study of a man who was blind as a baby but recovered sight by operation in middle life (see chapter 11). Shortly after the operation he thought he could lower himself safely to the ground from his hospital window, at least twelve metres above the ground. Although he saw the ground as just below him, his appreciation of familiar horizontal distances was quite accurate. Like the Zulus, he did not suffer from any of the normal illusions except, to a small degree, the arrow illusion.

The arrow illusion has been measured in some animals, notably the pigeon, and in fish. The technique is to train the experimental animals to select the longer of two lines, and when this is established, to present them with arrow figures in which the shafts are objectively equal. Do they then select the arrow which appears the longer to us? Positive results have been reported, both for pigeons and for the fish. It thus seems that animals are subject to the illusions.

(In fact this experiment is not as easy as it sounds, for it is important to establish that the animal is responding to the length of the shaft of the arrow and not to the length of the entire figure. This is done by training the animals with lines having various shapes added to their ends, to ensure that it is the length of the lines themselves and not the total length of the figures, which is being selected by the animals. In the training period, care is taken to use no additions to the lines which would produce an illusion. This is no doubt a hazardous experiment.)

The evidence from non-Western cultures in which there is little perspective (though there will always be some, if only perspective through motion parallax giving 'dynamic perspective') shows that the illusions are reduced, and largely absent, where perspective cues are meagre. The evidence from the man blind since infancy also suggests that illusions depend in part on previous visual experience. The evidence from animals suggests that illusions are not limited to the human perceptual system, but occur also in less developed eyes and brains. It would be interesting to bring animals up in a perspective-free environment and then measure their illusions. We might expect illusions to be absent. In fact, this experiment was tried in the author's laboratory, on fish. But unfortunately they died, though presumably not for perceptual reasons.

In connection with the non-Western people, it is perhaps worth adding that they make little or nothing of drawings or photographs of familiar objects, and this was also true of the blind man made to see. It is likely that perspective cues are made use of only after considerable experience, when they are related to touch, and that it is only then that appropriate perspective cues give rise to distortions of size in flat figures. There is some evidence that the illusion figures give rise to distortions of size as judged by touch. This is apparently true also of blind people touching these figures. The evidence for this is primarily on the arrow illusion, but this is perhaps not the best one to consider, for error of judged length in this figure could be due to the limited spatial acuity of the sense of touch tending to place the end of the line beyond the corner in the outgoing fins figure, and before the corner in the ingoing fins figure – so lengthening the first and shortening the second. As we have seen (in discussing the limited acuity theory) this is a most implausible explanation for illusions as *seen*, because of the high acuity of the eye; but it might be the explanation for touch where acuity is so low that the corners of the arrow figures may be displaced for this reason. This would be trivial. J. Frisby has recently provided evidence that people with vivid visual imagery tend to have greater than usual touch illusions. Is there a tie-up between touch and visual processing – as we suppose from evolution? Possibly touch information is interpreted according to visual 'models' of the world – and distorted by *visual* scaling processes.

# 10 Art and reality

Perspective as we know it in Western art is extraordinarily recent. In all known primitive art, and in the art of all previous civilisations, there is no perspective until the Italian Renaissance. In the highly developed formalised painting of the ancient Egyptians, heads and feet are shown in profile, never foreshortened by perspective; which gives the figures a certain resemblance to child art. Chinese drawing and painting is most curious in this respect, for distance is represented by formal rules which contravene geometry, and which often give what we would regard as reversed perspective – lines diverging rather than converging with increasing distance. It is an extraordinary fact that simple geometrical perspective took so long to develop – far longer than fire or the wheel – and yet in a sense it has always been present for the seeing. But is perspective present in nature? Is perspective a discovery, or an invention of the Renaissance artists?

The laws and principles of perspective were first clearly described by Leonardo da Vinci (1452–1519) in his *Notebooks*, where he outlines a suitable course of study for the artist including, as well as perspective, the arrangement of surface muscles, the structure of the eyes of man and animals, and botany. He called perspective 'the bridle and rudder of painting,' describing it in the following way:

> Perspective is nothing else than the seeing of a plane behind a sheet of glass, smooth and quite transparent, on the surface of which all the things approach the point of the eye in pyramids, and these pyramids are intersected on the glass plane.

Leonardo treated the perspective of drawings as a branch of geometry. He described how perspective could actually be drawn directly on a sheet of glass; a technique used by the Dutch masters and, in a later form, with the *camera obscura* which employs a lens to form an image of the scene which may be traced directly. The projection is determined purely by the geometry of the situation and this constitutes so-called *geometrical perspective;* but as Leonardo realised more clearly than many later writers, there is

10·1 This Canaletto is a fine example of perspective. It is worth pondering: has he painted the geometrical perspective, as given in the image in his eye, or has he painted the scene as he saw it – after his size constancy scaling has compensated for shrinkage of the image with distance? The question could be answered by photographing this scene and comparing the painting with the geometrical perspective given by the photograph.

10·2 An Egyptian scene. The figures are shown in characteristic positions and without perspective. Perspective was not introduced into art until the Italian Renaissance.

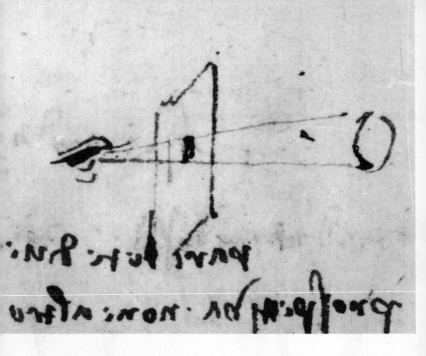

more to the matter than the pure geometry of the situation. Leonardo included in his account of perspective such effects as increasing haze and blueness with increasing distance; the importance of shadows and shading in drawings to represent the orientation of objects. These considerations go beyond pure geometry. But, as we shall see, they are highly relevant to the use of perspective, being essential to prevent its being ambiguous.

Any perspective projection is ambiguous – correct perspective may be a necessary but is never a sufficient condition for indicating depth. Consider a simple ellipse, such as in figure 10·6. This might represent an elliptical object seen normally or a circular object seen obliquely. This figure does not uniquely indicate any one kind of object: it could be a projection of any of an infinite variety of objects, each seen from a certain angle of view. The art of the draughtsman and painter is, in large part, to make us accept just one out of the infinite set of possible interpretations of a figure, to make us see a certain shape from a certain point of view. This is where geometry goes out and perception comes in. To limit the

10·3 Leonardo's sketch showing how three-dimensional objects appear on a flat plane.

**169**

ambiguity of perspective, the artist must make use of perceptual distance cues available to a single eye. He is forbidden the binocular cues of convergence and disparity, and also motion parallax. Indeed these cues will work against him. Paintings are generally more compelling in depth when viewed with a single eye, and the head held still.

We have to consider a double reality. The painting is itself a physical object, and our eyes will see it as such, flat on the wall, but it can also evoke quite other objects – people, ships, buildings – lying in space. It is the artist's task to make us reject the first reality, while conveying the second, so that we see his world and not mere patches of colour on a flat surface.

As we have seen from the example of the ellipse, a figure can represent a given object from one viewing position, or any of an infinite set of somewhat different objects seen in some other orientations. This means that for the figure to represent something unambiguously, we must know what the object really is – what its shape is – or how it lies in space. It is very much easier to represent familiar than unfamiliar objects. When we know what the object is, then we know how it must be lying to give the projection given by the artist. For example, if we know that the ellipse is representing a circular object, then we know that this must be lying at a certain oblique angle – the angle giving the eccentricity drawn on the flat plane by the artist. We all know that wheels, dinner plates, the pupil of the human eye, etc., are circular objects, and for such familiar objects the artist's task is easy. We may see how easy it is from the power that very simple line drawings have in indicating form, orientation and distance – when we know what the object is. Consider the drawing of the boy with the hoop in the cartoon (figure 10·7). It is quite clear that the ellipse represents a circle at an oblique angle, because we know that it represents a hoop, and we know that hoops are circular. The hoop in this figure is in fact the same as the ellipse seen without context in figure 10·6. But now we know what it is; we know how to see it. It would have been far more difficult for the artist to have represented a distorted hoop.

10·4 Chinese 'perspective'. This is very odd, for it is neither geometrical nor as the world appears through constancy scaling. Presumably the Chinese adopted highly conventionalised symbolic representation.
10·5 (*Right*). An early example of perspective:
*The Annunciation* by Crivelli (*c.* 1430–95).

OPVS CARO
LI CRIVELL
VENETI

LIBERTAS ✠ ECCLESIASTICA

Look at the amoeboid shape of the spilled wine in figure 10·8. It is seen as lying on a flat surface (the road), although the shape alone could equally well represent an infinity of shapes lying in various orientations. Suppose we remove the rest of the drawing, so that we have no clue as to what it represents. Figure 10·9 shows just the puddle. It could equally well be something of rather indeterminate shape standing up and facing us. (Does it not look slightly higher in the full drawing where it is clearly a puddle lying on the ground, than when it is an indeterminate shape? Does the context provide constancy scaling?) Although the figure is so simple it is evoking vast experience of objects – especially of what happens when we drop bottles – and this physical knowledge determines how we see the amoeboid shape.

We may now take another example, again of an ellipse in a cartoon, but this one illustrates a rather different point. Take the ellipse shape in figure 10·10. This is of some interest, for it is presented without any perspective, and yet it clearly lies on the floor. It is seen as a circle. The child below could be cutting an elliptical hole, but we assume he is cutting a circle, and this puts our viewing position at a certain height above ground which is not determined by any other feature in the drawing, but only by our interpretation

10.8 and 10.9 The puddle below is clearly lying flat on the ground – this is what puddles do. (*Right*) The same shape as the puddle in the cartoon, but how does it lie in space? It could be upright.

of the meaning of the shape based on our knowledge of small boys.

*When an artist employs geometrical perspective he does not draw what he sees – he represents his retinal image.* As we know, these are very different, for what is seen is effected by constancy. A photograph represents the retinal image, not how the scene appears. By comparing a drawing with a photograph taken from exactly the same position, we could determine just how far the artist adopts perspective and how far he draws the world as he sees it after his retinal images are scaled for his constancy. In general, distant objects look too small in a photograph – it is a common and sad experience that a grand mountain range comes out looking like a pitiful row of mole hills.

The situation here is curious. The camera gives true geometrical perspective, but because we do not see the world as it is projected on the retina, or a camera, the photograph looks wrong. It should not surprise us that primitive people make little or nothing of photographs. Indeed it is fortunate that perspective was invented before the camera, or we might have had great difficulty in accepting photographs as other than weird distortions. As it is, photographs can look quite wrong, particularly when the camera is not held horizontally. Aiming a camera upwards, to take in a tall building, gives the impression of the building falling backwards. And yet this is the true perspective. Skyscrapers do look slightly converging, though not so much as in a photograph taken from the same position and with the camera tilted at the same angle as the eyes. Some architects have recognised that the visual compensa-

tion for distance is less efficient when looking upwards, and have built their towers to diverge slightly from the bottom to the top The most notable example is the magnificent Campanile at Florence, designed by Giotto. Here the artist as architect has applied reversed perspective to reality, to compensate for the eye's inadequacy in correcting for perspective. There are examples of this on the horizontal plane also, notably the Piazza San Marco in Venice which is not a true rectangle but diverges towards the cathedral, so that it appears to be a true rectangle when the cathedral is viewed from across the Piazza. We find similar 'distortions' of reality to suit the eye and brain in some of the temples of ancient Greece.

We begin to see why it took so long for perspective to be adopted by painters. In an important sense perspective representations of three dimensions are wrong, for they do not depict the world as it is seen but rather the (idealised) images on the retina. But we do not see our retinal images; and we do not see the world according to the size or shapes of the retinal images, for these are effectively modified by Constancy. Should not the artist ignore perspective and draw the world as he sees it?

If the artist ignores perspective altogether his painting or drawing will look flat, unless indeed he can utilise other cues to distance with sufficient force. This seems to be almost impossible. If he did succeed in suggesting depth by other means, then the picture would again look wrong, for these other cues would trigger the viewer's Constancy system to expand the more distant objects as represented. This means that the artist should use perspective – draw distant objects smaller – if the viewer's Constancy scaling is affected by the depth cues he provides. Indeed, if he could provide all the normal depth cues, he should use complete perspective so that the viewer sees sizes and distances as though he were seeing the original three-dimensional scene. But – and this is the important point – in fact the artist cannot hope to provide all the depth cues present in reality, and so he should use a modified perspective.

10·10 Another ellipse. This time we assume it is a circle, and see it as flat, because we know that the boy under the floor (almost seen!) would generally saw a circular hole.

10·11 Impossible? We accept that the room is rectangular though in fact it is not, and see the figures as different sizes. This is what happens inside the Ames distorted room. We are so used to rooms being rectangular that we bet on the room being normal. Here we are wrong.

recedes from the observer (and the camera) to the left. The figure on the left is
further away, but the walls and windows are arranged to give the same retinal
image as a normal rectangular room, and the figures appear the same distance and
different sizes. (The nearer figure is about doubled in size in this room.)

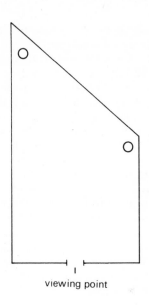

viewing point

## The Ames perspective demonstrations

An American psychologist, A. Ames, who started life as a painter,
produced a series of most ingenious and striking perceptual
demonstrations. Most famous is his Distorted Room. This is an
oddly shaped box, which may be the full size of a normal room.
The further wall is sloped back at one side, so that it does not lie
normal to the observer, but perspective is used to make this oddly
shaped room give the same retinal image as a normal rectangular
room. Now just as there is always an infinite set of arrangements
of objects and orientations which could give a particular retinal
image, so there is an infinite set of distorted rooms which could
give the same images as those of a normal rectangular room.

What does an Ames distorted room look like? It looks like a
normal rectangular room! There is really nothing surprising in

this: it *must* look like a normal room if constructed according to strict perspective, and viewed from the right position – because the image it gives is the same as for an ordinary room. But if now we place objects in the room, very odd things happen. An object placed at the further corner shrinks. It looks too small because the image is smaller than would be expected for the apparent distance of that part of the room. In this way an adult may be shrunk to appear smaller than a tiny child (figure 10·11). It is important that this effect still works in the photograph. In fact one does not really need the room to get the effect, for the photograph gives the same retinal image as the room, except that the photograph has, in addition, the flat-plane texture of the page.

Evidently we are so used to rectangular rooms that we accept it as axiomatic that it is the objects – the adult and the child – which are odd sizes, rather than that the room is an odd shape. But this is essentially a betting situation – it *could* be either, or both, which are peculiar. Here the brain makes the wrong bet, for the experimenter has rigged the odds. Indeed, perhaps the most interesting feature of the Ames Distorted Room is its implication that perception is a matter of making the best bet on the available evidence. It has been reported that wives may not see their husbands distorted by the Room – they see their husbands as normal, and the room its true queer shape. Behold the power of love?

To recapitulate: the empty Ames Distorted Room tells us nothing about perception. If properly constructed, it must look like a normal rectangular room giving the same projection from the observer's point of view. It must also look the same to a camera, or to any conceivable optical device or other kind of eye which does not get information of distance by other means. But when objects (such as people) are added, the room brings out the point that perceptual interpretation involves betting on the odds. The extreme distortion of a room is so unlikely (at least to Western eyes) that perception goes wrong when the truth is unlikely. This tells us something about the importance of previous experience and learning in perception. It is only familiar objects (husbands) which

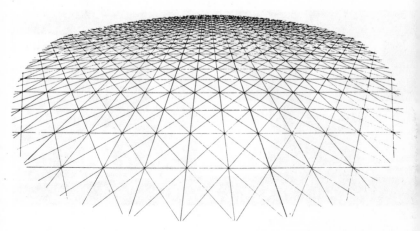

refuse to be distorted by the room. Familiarity with the room, especially through touching its walls, even with a stick held in the hand, does gradually reduce its distorting effect on other objects, and finally it comes to look more or less as it is – distorted in fact.

Another celebrated Ames demonstration is the Rotating Window. This is a flat, non-rectangular window-like object, made to rotate slowly by means of a small motor. It has shadows painted upon it (so that as it rotates the light source apparently casting the painted shadows has to rotate with it, in an unlikely way, since the 'shadows' on the 'window' never change in length). What is seen is a complex series of illusions. The direction of rotation is ambiguous, seeming to change spontaneously. (This is the 'windmill effect, observed when the rotating vanes are seen angled against the sky. The direction of rotation reverses spontaneously while one looks at it.) Any small object attached to the rotating window will suddenly seem to move in the wrong direction, when its movement is seen correctly though the window is seen falsely. The window may change dramatically in size – a remarkable and striking effect – seeming to expand in an impossible way. Evidently

10·14 A cunning trick which upsets depth.
The two sets of squares, though they
look the same, are differently arranged
in distance. In the third row of
playing cards, the jack is in fact
nearer than the six.

constancy has been upset by the atypical transformations at the eye
of this unlikely window. The demonstration is very dramatic
but too complicated to be a good research tool.

## Gibson's gradients

The work of J. J. Gibson, particularly on the perception of depth,
is justly celebrated. Gibson examines in particular the importance
of texture gradients (figure 10·13), and motion parallax, in determining apparent distance. He has throughout stressed the importance of considering real out-of-door situations He also
considers (in his later writings) that adequate analyses of the effects
of various patterns of retinal stimulation should be sufficient to
explain perception: he argues against neurological or cybernetic
models of perceptual processes supposed to be going on in the
brain. His approach is thus different from ours.

Gibson has designed many elegant experiments on situations
compelling depth, particularly the cue emphasised by Helmholtz
– the hiding of further by nearer objects, which is so powerful that
it can challenge and beat stereoscopic depth. One of Gibson's

10·15 The apparatus for producing the effect opposite. The nearer square and the playing card are cut away so as not, in fact, to overlap the more distant square and card. This is so unlikely that the distant and further squares and cards are reversed in distance. This shows that overlap of further by nearer objects is an important depth cue, and it involves some knowledge of the world of objects.

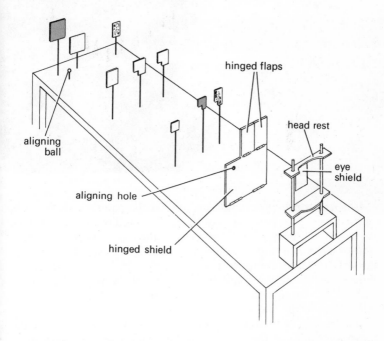

most beautiful demonstrations is to make the *further* object apparently overlap and partly cover the *nearer* – using playing cards with parts cut out, as in figure 10·14.

By pitting one cue against another (by reversing some, using such tricks as optically reversing the eyes, or Gibson's trick with the playing cards) it is possible to estimate the relative importance of the various cues in giving depth, including the so-called aerial perspective of atmospheric haze, making distant objects bluer and less distinct, described by Leonardo, Helmholtz and others.

It should be possible to get measures of the power of the various depth cues by employing the new technique described in the last chapter which gives objective measures of apparent depth.

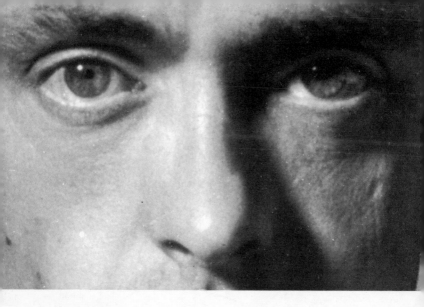

It is not at present at all clear how far the painter uses the cues normally used for perception of the world, and how far he develops devices which become effective cues to the *cognoscenti*, but which do not appear in nature or are not used by the eyes. It should be possible to learn about normal perception by studying the techniques and the failures and successes of artists, while they might learn a little by considering in more detail the problems of how we see objects in the real world.

If a drawing or photograph is presented without the texture of the paper on which it lies – by back-illumination of a photographic transparency in an otherwise dark room – then the perspective or other depth features of the drawing will cause it to be seen in astonishing depth, as though it were stereoscopic. Normally, the painter is in large measure defeated by his canvas, but it should not be beyond the wit of scientists to help him, should he wish to avoid the paradox of depth suggested but not truly seen in pictures.

## Shading and shadows

When working with line alone, much use is made of shading to indicate distance and orientation of objects. Shading may be used to indicate how an object lies by indicating texture. The shading is

10·16 Two viewing positions from one camera angle – the shadow shows the profile of the nose and eyes.

185

often conventional stippling or equally-spaced lines indicating a flat plane, unequal spacing indicating that the surface is irregular in depth.

Shading may also indicate shadow, and this is a different matter from regularity of surface texture. Shadows indicate the direction of light falling on the objects, and also where a second object obstructs the light. The shadow may be cast by overhanging features of an object – as when texture is revealed by shadow – and then both the texture of the surface and the direction of the illumination is indicated by the form and direction of the shadows. This is a matter of surprising importance. Shadows are important for they supplement the single eye, to give something surprisingly close to binocular depth. The light-source revealed by the shadows replaces the missing eye of the painter.

Consider a portrait taken full face, but with strong side lighting. The profile form of the nose is actually shown on the cheek (figure 10·16). The shadow thus gives us a second view of the nose. We get the same effect when looking at the moon through a telescope – indeed our knowledge of the profiles of the crater walls and the lunar mountains depends upon seeing their shadows cast by oblique sunlight. It is possible to measure the lengths of the shadows, and deduce accurately the height and form of lunar mountains. But the perceptual system does just this most of the time – and the world looks flat when the light is behind us and there are no shadows.

We have already noted that perceived depth can be reversed by interchanging the eyes optically, each eye receiving the normal view of the other (see chapter 4). Interestingly enough, reversal in depth given by the light-source 'eye' casting shadows, can also occur if it is shifted from its usual position. The point is that light normally falls from above: the sun cannot shine from below the horizon, and artificial light is generally placed high. When, however, illumination is from below, we tend to get reversed depth, just as though our eyes were switched over.

This effect was noted by several early writers: David Brewster

10·17 (*Top*) A moon model, with mountains and craters shown in depth by their shadows. (*Bottom*) The same moon model, but the other way up. Now what was a mountain may appear a depression: the direction of the shadows indicates different depth.

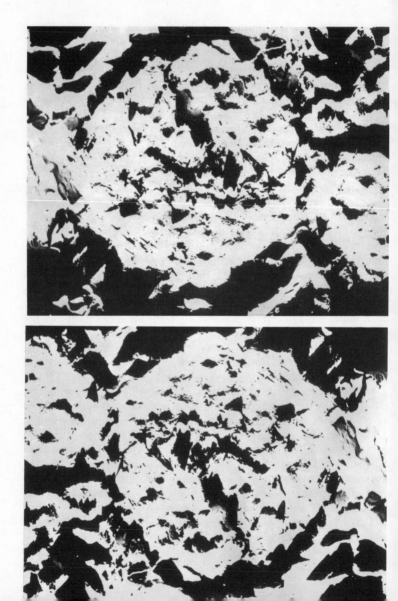

10·18 Letters? These are merely shadows, but we see the objects which would    187
cast the shadows. Look carefully: there are not really raised letters casting
the shadows, though we 'see' them. The brain sometimes invents objects to try
to make sense of what is presented to the eye.

# SHADOW

(1781–1868) records it in his *Letters on Natural Magic*, where he
describes how, when the direction of light falling upon a medal is
changed from above to below, depressions become elevations and
elevations depressions – i.e. intaglios become cameos and *vice
versa*. This was observed at an early meeting of the Royal Society,
by a member who was looking at a guinea coin through a microscope. Brewster said of it:

> The illusion . . . is the result of the operation of our own minds, whereby
> we judge the forms of bodies by the knowledge we have acquired of light
> and shadow.

He then goes on to experiment with the effect, finding it more marked
in adults than in children. He found that visual depth may become
reversed even when true depth is indicated by touch. This must
rank as one of the earliest psychological experiments. We now
know that chickens are subject to the same effect, and for them at
least it is innate.

The effect can occur when observing the moon through a telescope. It might even be a perceptual hazard in space travel, when
judging a lunar landing (figure 10·17).

Although shadows are joined to and so are part of objects, they
are normally quite distinct and are seldom confused with objects.
Shadows are so powerful perceptually that they can evoke perception of objects even when there are no objects present. This is
very clear in the typeface in figure 10·18. Here we see letters as
large as life, but in fact only the shadows of imaginary letters are
present. Could this effect, sometimes, make us see ghosts – figures
perceptually invented to 'explain' shadows?

11·1 The 'visual cliff'. This experiment, designed by Mrs Eleanor Gibson, subjects babies or young animals to a drop under a glass sheet.
The baby refuses to crawl on the glass, over the drop, and so evidently sees the depth and the danger.

# 11 Do we have to learn how to see?

A most ancient question in philosophy is: How do we come to know the world? Indeed, philosophies are divided into those branded as metaphysical – which hold that we are born with some knowledge of the world – and those of the empiricists who claim that all knowledge is derived from sensory experience. To the metaphysician, it is clear that by sitting in an armchair and thinking sufficiently hard, and in the right kind of way, it is possible to make discoveries about the world – even such discoveries as the number of planets – without having to get up and take a look. To empiricists this claim is nonsense: to know we must observe.

For 2,000 years metaphysicians upheld their claim by pointing to mathematics, especially geometry, where new facts were continually discovered not by experiment or by observation, but by thinking and juggling with symbols. It is only within the last century that it has become clear that mathematical discoveries are of a special kind: constituting knowledge not of objects, but of the allowed arrangements of the symbols. Mathematical discoveries are about mathematics, not about the world. We know that there is not but one possible geometry: other geometries can be invented, and it is an empirical question which best fits our world. Mathematics is useful in making explicit the steps of an argument; in making the steps between problem and conclusion automatic – given that a suitable method has been found – and in presenting data in convenient forms. But mathematics does not give new facts about the world in the sense that facts are discovered by observation.

There are, however, many animals which seem to know a lot about the world of objects before ever they experience it. Insects play successful hide-and-seek with predator and prey before they have time to learn. Migrating birds use the pattern of the stars to guide them over featureless oceans, even when they have never seen the sky. How can these things happen if the empiricists are right and all knowledge is derived from the senses?

Experimental psychology has grown up from philosophy and the smoke and the ashes of ancient controversy cling to it still. Psychologists distinguish between innate and learned responses; the former implying knowledge without previous experience, the latter knowledge from observation. But the issue in psychology is not the same as it was to the philosophers. To philosophers the question is: Can we know before we have perceived? To the psychologist the question is: Can we perceive before we have learned how to perceive? These questions are often confused, but they are really very different. It is only the second, the psychologists' question, which concerns us. Certainly insects and birds can respond appropriately to some objects upon first encounter, but this does not make them metaphysicians. They are heirs, by inheritance, to a state of knowledge won by ancestral disasters.

What is learned by an individual cannot be directly inherited by its descendants, but the genetic coding can become modified, by natural selection, to give the capacity to respond appropriately to objects, or situations, encountered for the first time by the individual. Patterns of behaviour, and the ability to recognise objects such as long-standing enemies, is as important to the survival of a creature as is its structure. Indeed, the limbs and the senses are useless unless they are used to effect: just as useless as tools without the skill to guide and direct them. Just as the simple reflexes serve, without learning, to protect a young animal from danger of falling, or being suffocated, so inborn perceptual skills may protect him from danger.

Animals low down on the evolutionary scale rely almost entirely upon unlearned perception of objects. But their perceptual range is small, and they respond only in stereotyped ways. Some insects do show perceptual learning, but the emphasis is upon 'innate' knowledge, learning being restricted largely to the whereabouts of their hive, or other shelter, so that they can return to base after foraging operations. The bee does not have to learn about flowers. The bee sucks where her ancestors found nectar – for by nectar they survived. The pattern of the petals leading to nectar became built into the bee's brain, as those without it died for lack of honey.

Given that structure develops by natural selection, it is not surprising that the same is true for behaviour, and perception.

What would be truly surprising in an empiricist view of nature, would be to find immediate 'recognition' of artificial or unimportant shapes. For example, if a child was found to recognise a language without having been taught it, this would be startling, for the knowledge could not have become genetically coded. But there is no good evidence for this kind of innate immediate knowledge. The point here may seem obvious, but not so long ago metaphysicians did indeed seriously hold that by pure thought the number of the planets could be known without the need for observation. It was this assumption that seemed obvious, while the empiricist's position seemed absurd and to flout the facts.

## Recovery from infant blindness

In man there is a long period of helpless infancy. During this time, just because the infant is almost entirely passive and cannot respond appropriately, it is extremely difficult to discover how much he perceives of the world. The question that confronts the psychologist is just what the human infant has to learn and what is given innately. The great American psychologist William James, described the world of the baby as 'a blooming, buzzing confusion' but is this so? How can we find out what the visual world of the baby is like? This question has engaged the attention of philosophers who have been fascinated by the possibility that one might learn how a baby comes to see, by asking a man born blind what happens to him upon recovery of sight. It is, of course, rare for a blind man to recover sight, but there are some cases, as we shall see in a moment.

The experience of the blind man was considered by Descartes, in the *Dioptrics*. Descartes considers how a blind man discovers the world by tapping with a stick. He says:

... without long practice this kind of sensation is rather confused and dim; but if you take men born blind, who have made use of such sensations all their life, you will find they feel things with such perfect exactness that one might almost say that they see with their hands.

The implication is that this kind of learning might be necessary for the normal child to develop his world of sight.

John Locke (1632–1704) received a celebrated letter from Molyneux, which posed the question:

> Suppose a man born blind, and now adult, and taught by his touch to distinguish between a cube and sphere of the same metal. Suppose then the cube and sphere were placed on a table, and the blind man made to see: query, whether by his sight, before he touched them, could he distinguish and tell which was the globe and which the cube? ... The acute and judicious proposer answers: not. For though he has obtained the experience of how the globe, how the cube, affects his touch so or so, must affect his sight so or so. . . .

Locke comments as follows:

> I agree with this thinking gentleman, whom I am proud to call my friend, in his answer to this his problem; and am of the opinion that the blind man, at first, would not be able with certainty to say which was the globe, which the cube . . .

Here we have a suggested psychological experiment. Previously a matter of philosophical speculation – now it becomes the subject of experimental enquiry.

George Berkeley (1685–1753) the Irish philosopher, also considered the problem. He says:

> In order to disentangle our minds from whatever prejudices we may entertain with the relation to the subject in hand nothing is more apposite than the taking into our thoughts the case of one born blind, and afterwards, when grown up, made to see. And though perhaps it may not be an easy task to divest ourselves entirely of the experience received from sight so as to be able to put our thoughts exactly in the posture of such a one's: we must nevertheless, as far as possible, endeavour to frame conceptions of what might reasonably be supposed to pass in his mind.

Berkeley goes on to say that we should expect such a man not to know anything was

> high or low, erect or inverted . . . for the objects to which he had hitherto used to apply the terms up and down, high and low, were such only as

affected or were some way perceived by his touch; but the proper objects of vision make new sets of ideas, perfectly distinct and different from the former and which can by no sort make themselves perceived by touch.

Berkeley then goes on to say that his opinion is that it would take some time to learn to associate touch with vision. This is a clear statement of the need for experience in infancy before perception is possible, which is generally stressed by empiricist philosophers.

There have been several actual cases of the sort imagined by Molyneux. The most famous is that of a thirteen-year-old boy described by Cheseldon, in 1728. There are altogether some sixty recorded cases, ranging from one in 1020 to the case of a man blind from ten months to fifty-two years of age, investigated by the present author and a colleague, Jean Wallace, a few years ago.

Some of the reported cases are much as the empiricist philosophers expected. They could see but little at first, being unable to name or distinguish between even simple objects or shapes. Sometimes there was a long period of training before they came to have useful vision, which indeed in many cases was never attained. Some gave up the attempt and reverted to a life of blindness, often after a period of severe emotional disturbance. On the other hand, some did see quite well almost immediately, particularly those who were intelligent and active, and who had received a good education while blind. The overall difficulty which these people have in naming the simplest objects by sight, and the slowness in the development of perception, so impressed the Canadian psychologist D. O. Hebb that he gave a lot of weight to this evidence, suggesting that indeed it shows how important perceptual learning is to the human infant.

It is important to note, however, that the reported cases do not all show extreme difficulty, or slowness, in coming to see. We should also remember that the operation itself is bound to disturb the optics of the eye, so that we cannot expect a reasonable image until the eye has had time to settle down after the operation. This is perhaps particularly important in the case of the removal of the lens for cataract, which constitutes all the earlier cases, while the other kind of operable blindness – opacity of the cornea – involves somewhat less profound damage to the eye as a whole. The cases of corneal grafting are all comparatively recent: the case which I had the good fortune to investigate at first hand was of this kind.

### The case of S.B.

This case, a man of fifty-two, whom we may call S.B., was when blind, an active and intelligent man. He would go for cycle rides, with a friend holding his shoulder to guide him; he would often dispense with the usual white stick, sometimes walking into parked cars or vans and hurting himself as a result. He liked making things, with simple tools in a shed in his garden. All his life he tried to picture the world of sight: he would wash his brother-in-law's car, imagining its shape as vividly as he could. He longed for the day when he might see, though his eyes had been given up as hopeless, so that no surgeon would risk wasting a donated cornea. Finally the attempt was made, and it was successful. But though the operation was a success, the story ends in tragedy.

When the bandages were first removed from his eyes, so that he was no longer blind, he heard the voice of the surgeon. He turned to the voice, and saw nothing but a blur. He realised that this must be a face, because of the voice, but he could not see it. He did not suddenly see the world of objects as we do when we open our eyes.

But within a few days he could use his eyes to good effect. He could walk along the hospital corridors without recourse to touch; he could even tell the time from a large wall clock, having all his life carried a pocket watch having no glass, so that he could feel the time from its hands. He would get up at dawn, and watch from his window the cars and trucks pass by. He was delighted with his progress, which was extremely rapid.

When he left the hospital, we took him to London and showed him many things he never knew from touch, but he became curiously dispirited. At the zoo he was able to name most of the animals correctly, having stroked pet animals, and enquired as to how other animals differed from the cats and dogs he knew by touch.

He was also of course familiar with toys and models. He certainly used his previous knowledge from touch, and reports from sighted people to help him name objects by sight, which he did largely by seeking their characteristic features. But he found the world drab, and was upset by flaking paint and blemishes on things. He liked bright colours, but became depressed when the light faded. His depressions became marked, and general. He gradually gave up active living, and three years later he died.

Depression in people recovering sight after many years of blindness seems to be a common feature of the cases. Its cause is probably complex, but in part it seems to be a realisation of what they have missed – not only visual experience, but opportunities to do things denied them during the years of blindness. Some of the cases revert very soon to living without light, making no attempt to see. S.B. would often not trouble to turn on the light in the evening, but would sit in darkness.

We tried to discover what his visual world was like by asking him questions and giving him various simple perceptual tests. While still in the hospital, before he became depressed, he was most careful with his judgments and his answers. We found that his perception of distance was peculiar, and this is true of earlier cases. He thought he would just be able to touch the ground below his window with his feet if he lowered himself by his hands, but in fact the distance down was at least ten times his height. On the other hand, he could judge distances and sizes quite accurately provided he already knew the objects by touch. Although his perception was demonstrably peculiar, he seldom expressed surprise at anything he saw. He drew the elephant (figure 11·2) before we showed him one at the zoo, but upon seeing it he said immediately: 'there's an elephant,' and said it looked much as he expected it would. On one object he did show real surprise, and this was an object he could not have known by touch – the moon. A few days after the operation, he saw what he took to be a reflection in a window (he was for the rest of his life fascinated by reflections in mirrors and would spend hours sitting before a

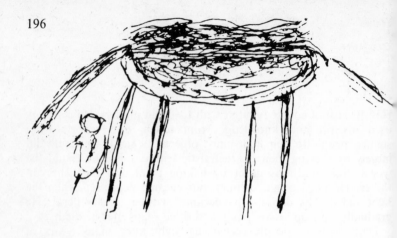

mirror in his local public house, watching people), but this time what he saw was not a reflection, but the quarter moon. He asked the Matron what it was, and when she told him, he said he thought the quarter moon would look like a quarter piece of cake!

S.B. never learned to read by sight (he read Braille, having been taught it at the blind school) but we found that he could recognise block capital letters, and numbers, by sight without any special training. This surprised us greatly. It turned out that he had been taught upper case, though not lower case, letters at the blind school. They were given raised letters on wooden blocks, which were learned by touch. Although he read upper case block letters immediately by sight, it took him a long time to learn lower case letters, and he never managed to read more than simple words. Now this finding that he could immediately read letters visually which he had already learned by touch, showed very clearly that he was able to use his previous touch experience for his new-found vision. This is interesting to the psychologist, for it indicates that the brain is not so departmentalised as is sometimes thought. But it makes any finding of these cases difficult or impossible to apply to the normal case of a human infant coming to see. The blind adult knows a great deal about the world of objects through touch and hearsay: he can use some of this information to help him identify objects from the slightest cues. He also has to come to accept and trust his new sense, which means giving up the habits of many years. His case is really quite unlike that of the child's.

S.B.'s use of early touch experience comes out clearly in drawings which he did for us, starting while still in the hospital and continuing for a year or more. The series of drawings of buses (in figure 11·3) illustrate how he was unable to draw anything he did not already know by touch. In the first drawing the wheels have spokes, and spokes are a distinctive touch feature of wheels. The windows seem to be represented as he knew them by touch, from the inside. Most striking is the complete absence of the front of the bus, which he would not have been able to explore with his hands, and which he was still unable to draw six months or even a year later. The gradual introduction of writing in the drawings indicates visual learning: the sophisticated script of the last drawing meant nothing to him for nearly a year after the operation, although he could recognise block capitals while still in the hospital, having learned them previously from touch. It seems that S.B. made immediate use of his earlier touch experience, and that for a long time his vision was very largely limited to what he already knew.

We saw in a dramatic form the difficulty that S.B. had in trusting and coming to use his vision whenever he had to cross the road. Before the operations, he was undaunted by traffic. He would cross alone, holding his arm or his stick stubbornly before him, when the traffic would subside as the waters before Christ. But after the operation, it took two of us on either side to force him across a road: he was terrified as never before in his life.

When he was just out of the hospital, and his depression was but occasional, he would sometimes prefer to use touch alone, when identifying objects. We showed him a simple lathe (a tool he had wished he could use) and he was very excited. We showed it him first in a glass case, at the Science Museum in London, and then we opened the case. With the case closed, he was quite unable to say anything about it, except that the nearest part might be a handle (which it was – the transverse feed handle), but when he was allowed to touch it, he closed his eyes and placed his hand on it when he immediately said with assurance that it was a handle. He ran his hands eagerly over the rest of the lathe, with his eyes

11·3 (Below) S.B.'s first drawing of a bus (48 days after the corneal graft operation giving him sight). All the features given were probably known to him by touch. The front, which he had not explored by touch, is missing, and he could not add it when we asked him to try. (*Top right*) Six months later. Now he adds writing, the 'touch' spokes of the wheels have been rejected, but he still cannot draw the front. (*Bottom right*) A year later he adds writing, but the front is still missing!

tight shut for a minute or so; then he stood back a little, and opening his eyes and staring at it he said: 'Now that I've felt it I can see.'

Although many philosophers and psychologists think that these cases can tell us about normal perceptual development in infants, I am inclined to think that they tell us rather little. As we have seen, the difficulty is essentially that the adult, with his great store of knowledge from the other senses, and reports from sighted people, is very different from the infant who starts with no knowledge from experience. It is extremely difficult, if not entirely impossible, to use these cases to answer Molyneux's question. The cases are interesting and dramatic, but when all is said, they tell us little about the world of the baby, for adults with restored vision are not living fossils of infants.

## Direct evidence from babies

To discover how much the human baby has to learn to see we must find other evidence. We must either find out directly what a baby can see, or discover more about how far adults can learn to see strange things. First, let us look at the evidence from the baby himself.

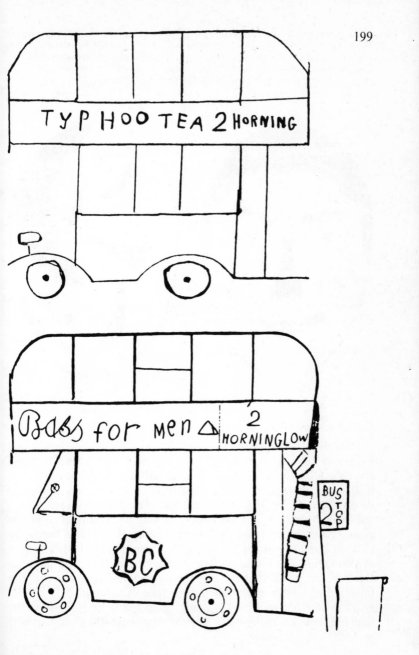

11·4 Fantz's apparatus (*right*) for observing babies' eye movements while they are shown various designs, or objects. Here the baby is shown an illuminated ball, while the eye positions are photographed. (*Below*) A simple face, and a randomised face-like design which were shown to very young babies. They spent longer looking at the true face picture (as judged by their eye movements).

### Babies' eye movements

A quite different approach to the problem of discovering how much babies see, has been developed recently by R. L. Fantz. He gets round the difficulty, so far as possible, that babies have almost no controlled movements, by using what little they have: the ability to direct the eyes to objects of interest. Fantz places very young babies comfortably on their backs, looking up, and then he places pairs of figures on large cardboard screens above their heads, so that the baby can direct his eyes upon them (figure 11·4). The eyes are observed, and photographed with a cine camera, and the time the eyes rest on each of the two figures is noted. He finds that the babies direct their eyes longer at a face-like design than at the random face design which is made up of the same lines. It seems that the face is a meaningful object to babies without any special

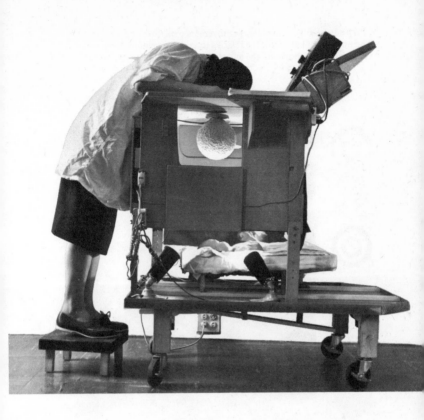

learning, and this is a new, simple and important discovery.

It is also found that babies seem to prefer simple round objects to flat representations of the same objects, suggesting that they may have some innate appreciation of depth.

These experiments may give direct evidence of immediate visual response to biologically important objects, but even this is not entirely certain, for the mother's face is not hidden, so it is possible that the early preference for face-like patterns is not truly innate but learned extremely rapidly, perhaps by association with the pleasures of the breast.

### The 'visual cliff'

Mrs Eleanor Gibson, while picnicking on the rim of the Grand Canyon, wondered whether a young baby would fall off. This

11·5 Some results of Fantz's eye movement experiments on babies. The horizontal bars show the relative times they spent looking at the various designs shown on the left of the diagram.

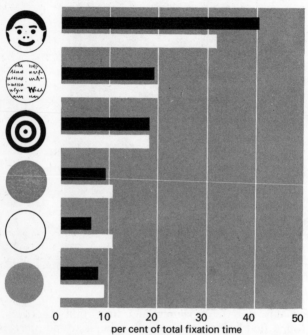

per cent of total fixation time

thought led her to a most elegant experiment, for which she devised a miniature and safe Grand Canyon. The apparatus is shown in figure 11·1, which shows a central 'bridge' with, on one side a normal solid floor, and over the drop a large sheet of strong glass. An infant (or in other experiments a young animal) is placed on the central bridge, and the question is: will he crawl on the glass over the drop? The answer is that the baby will not leave the bridge on the drop side, and cannot be enticed over it by his mother shaking his rattle, though he will crawl quite happily on to the normal floor on the other side of the bridge. It thus seems clear that babies at the crawling stage can visually appreciate a drop. The usefulness of this appreciation of dangerous heights is, however, somewhat reduced by the fact that they will sometimes forget where their legs are, so that they would fall off the cliff but for the transparent floor! They seem to appreciate depth from motion parallax.

## Displaced images

This is just about all that is known directly about the amount of perception in young babies. To pursue the matter of perceptual learning further, we must look at a quite different, and less direct, kind of evidence: how far can the adult human being adapt to bizarre changes in his visual world?

Before Kepler realised that the retinal image is upside down, due to the light crossing at the lens, Leonardo assumed that the light must cross at two places inside the eye (at the pupil and the vitreous humour) to give a right-way-up image. Presumably Leonardo felt that an upside-down image would make the world appear upside down. But would it?

The matter was discussed in detail by Helmholtz, who argued that it does not matter which way up the image is, providing it is systematically related to the outside world of objects, as known by touch and the other senses.

He believed that we have to learn to see the world, by relating visual sensations with touch, but that no special handicap is provided by the inversion of the image. Helmholtz supported his contention that early learning is important for perception by considering the cases of adults born blind but later gaining sight by operation. Helmholtz did not in fact get direct evidence for the learning of 'uprightness' in this way, but he did think that the difficulty many patients had in naming objects and judging distances provides evidence for his empiricist theory that perception depends on learning. We have seen some of the difficulties involved in interpreting these cases.

We may take up Helmholtz's suggestion that learning is required to see things the right way up by considering experiments in which the image has been deliberately inverted from its usual upside-down position.

### Inverted images

The experiments fall into two groups: those in which the position or orientation of the image is changed, and those in which the image is deliberately distorted. We will start with the classical work of the American psychologist, G. M. Stratton. He wore inverting lenses and was the first man in the world to have retinal images the right way up.

Stratton devised a variety of optical devices for displacing and inverting the retinal image. He used lens and mirror systems, including special telescopes mounted on spectacle frames so that they could be worn continuously. These lens systems inverted both vertically and horizontally. Stratton found that if a pair of inverting lens systems were worn to give binocular vision, the strain was too great, since normal convergence was upset. He therefore wore a reversing telescope on but one eye, keeping the other covered. When not wearing the inverting lenses he would keep his eyes covered. At first, although the inverted images were clear, objects seemed illusory and unreal. Stratton wrote:

> . . . the memory images brought over from normal vision still continued to be the standard and criterion of reality. Things were thus seen in one way and thought of in a far different way. This held true also for my body. For the parts of my body were felt to be where they would have appeared had the instrument (the inverting lenses) been removed; they were seen to be in another position. But the older tactual and visual localisation was still the real localisation.

Later, however, objects would sometimes look almost normal.

Stratton's first experiment lasted three days, during which time he wore the 'instrument' for about twenty-one hours. He concluded thus:

> I might almost say that the main problem – that of the importance of the inversion of the retinal image for upright vision – had received from the experiment a full solution. For if the inversion of the retinal image were absolutely necessary for upright vision . . . it is difficult to understand

how the scene as a whole could even temporarily have appeared upright when the retinal image was not inverted.

Objects only occasionally looked normal, however, and so Stratton undertook a second experiment with his monocular inverting arrangement, this time wearing it for eight days. On the *third day* he wrote:

Walking through the narrow spaces between pieces of furniture required much less care than hitherto. I could watch my hands as they wrote, without hesitating or becoming embarrassed thereby.

On the *fourth day* he found it easier to select the correct hand, which had proved particularly difficult.

When I looked at my legs and arms, or even when I reinforced my effort of attention on the new visual representation, then what I saw seemed rather upright than inverted.

By the *fifth day* Stratton could walk around the house with ease. When he was moving around actively, things seemed almost normal, but when he gave them careful examination they tended to be inverted. Parts of his own body seemed in the wrong place, particularly his shoulders which, of course, he could not see. But by the evening of the *seventh day* he enjoyed for the first time the beauty of the scene on his evening walk.

On the *eighth day* he removed the inverting spectacles, and found that

... the scene had a strange familiarity. The visual arrangement was immediately recognised as the old one of pre-experimental days; yet the reversal of everything from the order to which I had grown accustomed during the last week, gave the scene a surprising bewildering air which lasted for several hours. It was hardly the feeling, though, that things were upside down.

One has the impression when reading the accounts of Stratton, and the investigators who followed him, that there is always something queer about their visual world, though they have the greatest difficulty in saying just what is wrong with it. Perhaps rather than their inverted world becoming normal, they cease to notice how odd it is, until their attention is drawn to some special feature, when it does look clearly wrong. We read of such situations where writing appears in the right place in the visual field and at first sight looks like normal writing, except that when one attempts to read, it is seen as inverted.

Stratton went on to perform other experiments which though less well-known are just as interesting. He devised a mirror arrangement which, mounted in a harness (figure 11·6), visually displaced his own body, so that it appeared horizontally in front of him, and at the height of his own eyes. Stratton wore this mirror arrangement for three days (about twenty-four hours of vision) and he reported:

> I had the feeling that I was mentally outside my own body. It was, of course, but a passing impression, but it came several times and was vivid while it lasted. . . . But the moment critical interest arose, the simplicity of the state was gone, and my visible actions were accompanied by a kind of wraith of themselves in the older visual terms.

Stratton summed up his work in the following words:

> The different sense-perceptions, whatever may be the ultimate course of their extension, are organised into one harmonious spatial system. The harmony is found to consist in having our experiences meet our expectations. . . . The essential conditions of the harmony are merely those which are necessary to build up a reliable cross-reference between the two senses. This view, which was first based on the results with the inverting senses, is now given wider interpretation, since it seems evident from the later experiment that a given tactual position may have its correlated visual place not only in any direction, but also at any distance in the visual field.

Several investigators have followed up Stratton's work. G. C. Brown used prisms to rotate the field of both eyes through 75°, and found that while this reduced the efficiency of depth perception, there was little or no evidence that it improved with experience,

11·6 Stratton's experiment, in which he saw himself suspended in space before his eyes, in a mirror. He went for country walks wearing this arrangement.

though he and his subjects did find that they got used to their tilted world. Later studies are those of Ewert, who repeated Stratton's experiment but using a pair of inverting lenses, in spite of the strain on the eyes found by Stratton. Ewert's work has the great merit that he made systematic and objective measures of his subject's ability to locate objects. He concluded that Stratton somewhat exaggerated the amount of adaptation that occurred, and this led to a controversy that is still unresolved.

The problem was taken up by J. and J. K. Paterson, using a binocular system similar to Ewert's. After fourteen days they did not find complete adaptation to the situation. Upon re-testing the subject of the experiment eight months later, they found that when the lenses were worn, the subject immediately showed the various modifications to his behaviour which he previously developed

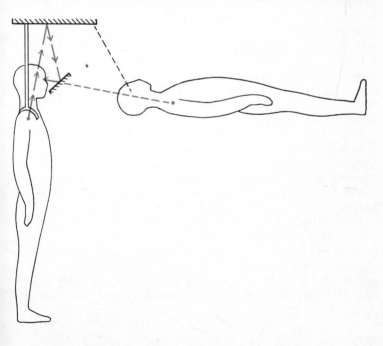

wearing the inverting spectacles. It thus seemed that the learning consisted of a series of specific adaptations overlying the original perception, rather than a reorganisation of the original perceptual system.

The most extensive recent experiments on humans have been carried out at Innsbruck by Erismann and Ivo Kohler.

Kohler and his subjects wore their reversing spectacles for long periods. Both Stratton's and Kohler's experiments rely on verbal reports. Kohler stresses the 'inner world' of perception following the European tradition which we find in the German Gestalt writers, and the more recent work of Michotte on the perception of causality (see chapter 12). The emphasis is foreign to the Behaviourist tradition of America, and certainly it is unfortunate that but little precise recording of the subject's movements during the experiments was attempted. From the verbal reports it is difficult to imagine the 'adapted' world of the experimental subjects, for their perceptions seem to be curiously shuffled and even paradoxical. For example pedestrians were evidently seen on the correct side of the street when the images were right-left reversed, though their clothes were seen as *the wrong way round*! Writing is one of the more puzzling kind of things observed. Writing would look normal when glanced at briefly, but it would appear as mirror-writing when attended to carefully.

Touch had important effects on vision: during the early stages of adaptation objects would tend to look suddenly normal when touched, and they would also tend to look normal when the reversed appearance was physically impossible. For example a candle would look upside down until lighted, when it would suddenly look normal, the flame going upwards.

These experiments gave place to several studies of animals fitted with goggles of various kinds. Inverting goggles placed on a monkey had the effect of immobilising her for several days, so that she simply refused to move. When she did finally move it was backwards – a point of some interest as these inverting goggles tend to reverse depth perception. Similar experiments have also been tried on chickens and hens. Right-left reversing prisms were attached to the eyes of hens by Pfister, who then observed their ability to peck grain. The hens were severely disturbed, and they showed no real improvement after three months wearing the prisms. This same lack of adaptation has also been found in amphibians investigated by Sperry. With their eyes rotated through 180°, it was found that they would move their tongue in the wrong direction for food, and they would have starved to death had they been left to fend for themselves. Similar results were also obtained by Hess, with chickens wearing prisms which did not reverse the images, but shifted them by 7°, either to the right or to the left. Hess found that these chickens would always peck to the side of grain, and that they never adapted to the shift of the image caused by the wedge prisms (figure 11·7). Hess concludes from these experiments:

> Apparently the innate picture which the chick has of the location of objects in its visual world cannot be modified through learning if what is required is that the chick learns to perform a response which is antagonistic to its instinctive one.

It seems quite clear from the various experiments, that animals show far less adaptation to shift or reversal of the image than do human observers. Indeed, only monkeys show any adaptation at all.

There is recent evidence, mainly from the work of R. Held and his associates, particularly A. Hein, to show that for compensation to displaced images to occur it is essential that the subject should make active corrective movements. Held considers that active movement is vital for such compensations, and also that it is essential for perceptual learning in the first place. One of his experimemts with kittens is particularly ingenious and interesting. He brought up kittens in darkness, allowing them vision only in the experimental situation – which was unusual to say the least. Two kittens were placed in baskets attached to opposite ends of a pivoted beam which could swing round its centre, while the baskets could also rotate. It was so arranged that a rotation of one basket caused the other to rotate similarly (the arrangement is seen

in figure 11·8) and so both kittens received very much the same visual experience, and at the same time. One of the kittens was placed in the basket so that it was carried passively, while the other kitten was active, for its limbs moved its own and its neighbour's basket. Held found that only the active kitten developed perception, the passive animal remaining effectively blind. He thus suggested that active touch is essential to perceptual development.

### Distorted images

Taken together, the work on inverted and displaced retinal images shows that animals lower than man and monkeys show no adaptation. Adaptation in monkeys is apparently very limited, and just how far adaptation occurs in man is still not entirely clear. The verbal reports are somewhat ambiguous, and there is little precise data on motor adaptation, though it is certain that people

11·8 Apparatus designed by Held and Hein to discover whether perceptual learning takes place in a passive animal. The kitten on the right is carried about by the active kitten on the left. They have similar visual input to the eyes. Only the active animal is able to perform visual tasks after visual experience limited to this situation.

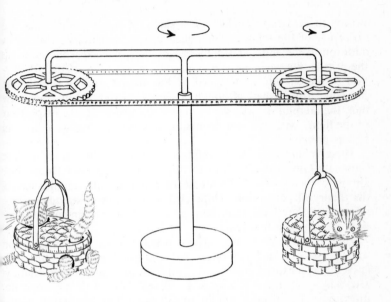

can cope quite well after a few days wearing inverting spectacles. We do not know for certain whether the adaptation is a re-organising of perception, or rather an overlaying of old responses by new ones. It is not even certain how much fundamental re-organisation is required, since we have had experience throughout our lives of displacement of retinal images due to tilting of the head and looking (mainly at ourselves) in mirrors.

So far we have considered experiments on inverting and tilting the images, but other kinds of disturbance can be produced. These are important because they involve some internal reorganisation in the perceptual system itself, rather than simple changes in the relation between the worlds of touch and vision. This can be done by wearing special lenses which distort, rather than displace, the image on the retina.

J. J. Gibson found, while undertaking an experiment wearing

prisms to deviate the field to one side (15° to the right), that the *distortion* of the image, which such prisms inevitably produce in addition to the shift, gradually became less marked while he wore the prisms. He went on to make accurate measures of the adaptation to the curvature produced by the prisms, and he found that the effect diminished although his eyes moved about freely. In fact, the adaptation was slightly more marked with free inspection of the figure with eye movements, than when the eyes were held as still as possible.

There is another kind of adaptation, at first sight similar to that found by Gibson with his distorting prisms, and later lenses, but almost certainly very different in its origin and its significance to the theory of perception. These effects are known as *figural after-effects* and they have received a great deal of experimental attention over the last few years.

Figural after-effects are induced when a figure is looked at for some time (say half a minute) with the eyes held very still. If a curved line is fixated in this way, a straight line viewed immediately afterwards will for a few seconds, appear curved in the opposite direction. The effect is similar to Gibson's, but for figural after-effects it is essential that the eyes should be still while with the distorting glasses effect of Gibson, the eyes can be moved freely about.

These effects show that adaptation can take place in the human perceptual system, and these adaptations are not only a simple readjustment between touch and vision, but can be a rescaling of visual space. There is no evidence as to whether such corrections occur in animals lower than man.

A remarkable discovery has been made recently by Ivo Kohler. He wore glasses which did not distort, but which were coloured half red and half green, so that everything looked red while looking to the left and green when looking to the right (figure 11·9). Kohler found a new adaptation effect, which could not have been anticipated. The effect of the colours gradually lessened, and when the glasses were removed, *things seen with the eyes directed to the right looked red, and to the left, green*. This effect is quite different

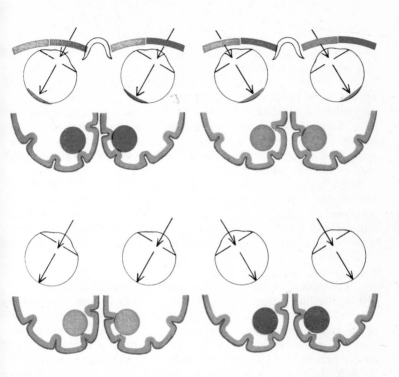

from the normal after-images due to adapting the retina to a coloured light. Kohler's effect was not related to the position of the image on the retina, but to the position of the eyes in the head, and so it must be due to a compensation taking place not in the eyes but in the brain.

There are severe limitations to the kinds of inversion possible by simple optical means, and recently a new technique has been adopted by K. U. Smith. Smith uses a television camera and monitor, so arranged that the subject watches his own hand on the monitor, which may be connected electronically to the camera to give any desired inversion.

It is a simple matter to give either left-right or up-down reversal of the image, and eye and hand movements are not affected. In this arrangement the hand is placed to the side of the subject, behind a curtain, so that it cannot be seen directly. (Since the apparatus is far from portable, the studies are limited to short experimental sessions, rather than to continuous reversal of many days' duration.) In addition to reversals, the camera may be placed in any position, giving a view displaced in space. Using various lenses and camera distances the size may be varied and distortions may be introduced (figure 11·10).

These techniques show that pure up-down reversal generally proves more disturbing than left-right reversal, though combined up-down left-right reversal was sometimes less disturbing than either alone. Changes in size had practically no effect on ability to draw objects, or on handwriting. Generally, adaptation was rapid.

### Displacement of images in time

An elaboration of the television technique makes it possible to displace retinal images not only in space, but in time. Temporal delay of images is a new kind of displacement, and promises to be of the greatest importance. The method is to use a TV camera and monitor as described above, but to introduce a video tape recorder between the camera and monitor, with an endless tape loop so that there is a time-delay between the recording from the camera and the play-back to the monitor. The subject thus sees his hands (or any other object) in the past; the delay being set by the gap between the Record and Play-back heads (figure 11·11) for time-displaced images.

This situation is not only of theoretical interest, but is also of practical importance because controls used in flying aircraft, and operating many kinds of machine, have a delay in their action: if such delay upsets the skill, this could be a serious matter. It was found that a short delay (about 0·5 seconds) made movements jerky and ill co-ordinated, so that drawing became almost impossible, and writing quite difficult (figure 11·12). Practice gives little or no improvement.

11·10 Smith's experiment, using a television camera and monitor to vary the viewing position or size of the subject's own hands. He can draw or write with large changes in the viewing position.

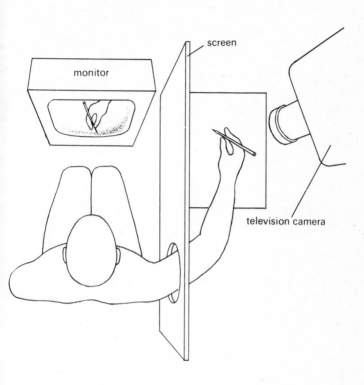

## What can we conclude?

We have had a look at experiments on displacements of various kinds of the retinal images. In all cases the displacements have been systematic, and a wide variety have been investigated: vertical and horizontal (either together or singly); distortions, either with or without free eye movements; and displacements in time.

The results are not too easy to assess, but broadly it seems that some adaptation does occur in humans to all these displacements

11·11 Smith's experiment, introducing time delay between acting and seeing. The delay is given by the tape loop of the video recorder.

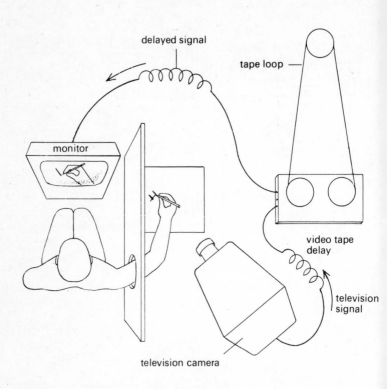

delayed signal

tape loop —

monitor

video tape delay

television signal

television camera

– except to time delay – while there is no evidence of any adaptation in animals lower than man except possibly for monkeys.

Does this show that human babies have to learn to see? It certainly does not prove it; but if it is indeed true that adults are capable of drastically modifying their perceptual system to compensate for systematic changes, then it at least makes it plausible to suppose that learning is important in the first place. Unfortunately, we do not know how far the adaptation is a basic reorganisation, and how far it is an overlaying of earlier by later

11·12 Drawing and writing with time delay. Left to right: normal, with TV    217
but no delay, with TV delay. The delay provides an insuperable handicap,
though displacement in space can be compensated. (The result is of practical
importance, since many control tasks, such as flying, do impose a delay
between action and result.)

perceptual interpretation. But in either case, it is evident that the human perceptual system is remarkably flexible and able to adapt to new conditions. Which is a good thing in a changing world.

Where adaptation does take place – as in the human experiments of Stratton and Gibson, where the image is inverted or distorted – it is not entirely clear that the world does come to look normal. It seems rather that its peculiarity is no longer noticed, and this is a different conclusion. In the experiments of Held where pairs of kittens were brought up in darkness, and only the active kitten of each pair learned to see – and also the earlier pioneering work of Reisen who brought up chimpanzees in total darkness and found but slow development of vision after being allowed the light – one might question the interpretations generally given.

Animals brought up in the dark are generally passive, and learn very little about anything. Some of the human cases of arrested vision seem to have been remarkably stupid – one of them was unable to differentiate between a sphere and a cube by *touch*! These experiments are interesting and important, but at the present time we cannot with safety go overboard on a precise statement of what they mean. It is clear that perception in man is susceptible to modification by learning (and indeed a medical student using the microscope for the first time knows this from his own experience), but it is very difficult to establish just what is given and what is learned in infancy.

To add to our difficulties in considering this matter, there is a curious and baffling logical difficulty which makes us question just what we should mean by 'perception', especially when interpreting animal experiments. To take for example Held's experiment with the active and passive kittens: suppose for a moment that the passive kitten *does* learn to see, in the sense that its patterns of retinal stimulation do become organised into separate objects, as it is carried around by its active partner. Now how could we know that the kitten had, in this sense, learned to see? How could he be expected to make appropriate responses if his behaviour had never become connected with his perception of objects? This raises a basic problem: should we think of perception as we know it in ourselves – *experience* of the world of objects – or should we limit its study to *behaviour*, under the control of sensory information? To the strict behaviourist, experience cannot be the subject-matter of perceptual studies: but we are bound to assume that in a concert hall or a picture gallery people experience an inner world, sufficiently important to draw them there. Whatever it is that art critics discuss, it is not the overt behaviour of the patrons of the arts, but rather what they experience. And yet can we talk about the perceptual experience of animals? Perhaps not, and this is the difficulty. Just as we do not understand the perceptual world of the baby, so we do not understand the perceptual world of animals; and whatever their behaviour, it seems insufficient as a guide. Language is specially important here: for language transcends the immediate situation of stimulus and overt responses; but in this instance language – and it has its pitfalls – is unavailable just when we need it most.

# 12 Seeing and believing

The sense organs receive patterns of energy, but we seldom see patterns: we see objects. A pattern is a relatively meaningless arrangement of marks, but objects have a host of characteristics beyond their sensory features. They have pasts and futures; they change and influence each other, and have hidden aspects which emerge under different conditions.

A brick and a block of gelignite may look and feel much alike, but they will behave very differently. We do not generally define objects by how they appear, but rather by their uses and their causal characteristics. A table may be one of many shapes, it is an object on which other objects may be placed, it may be square or round, or kidney-shaped, and still be a table. For a perception to correspond to an object – to be 'true' – certain expectations must be fulfilled. If a book were placed on a supposed table, which then melted away, or looked like an elephant, we would have to say that it was not, after all, a table. And also that there was not, after all, a perception; but a dream perhaps, or an hallucination. The importance of regular, lawful, relations in perceptions has been studied by Professor Michotte of Louvain, who has for many years investigated the perception of causality.

Michotte has studied the velocities and time-delays which are necessary for 'seeing' causality. He uses neutral moving patches of colour, generally produced with the apparatus shown in figure 12·1. He arranges one coloured patch to move towards and touch another which then moves off, generally after a small controlled delay. With some combinations of velocity and delay there is an irresistible impression that the first patch has struck the second, and pushed it, as though they were objects such as billiard balls. Indeed, one experiences just this effect in a cartoon film, and the objects in a cartoon can be abstract and still display the causal relations of real objects. Michotte is inclined to think that the seeing of cause is innately given, but this view seems to be based on the similarity of his different observers' verbal reports on their visual experience. There are obvious difficulties in arguing from such verbal reports – as Michotte would no doubt be the first to admit. Since we all experience much the same kinds of objects, we should expect similar velocity and delay characteristics to become reflected in perceptual appreciation of cause; and so agreement can hardly demonstrate that the perception of cause is innate rather than derived from experience of objects. Experiments on observers with long experience of unusual kinds of objects might give evidence of the importance of learning to see causes.

Although the sensory worlds of sight, touch and smell are very different from each other, we have no hesitation in accepting that they are alternative indications of the same world of objects. But our knowledge of the world of objects is certainly not limited to sensory experience: we know about magnetism although we cannot sense it, and about atoms although they are invisible.

It seems that the retina of the frog is capable of signalling only a few characteristics; mainly movement and the presence of corners. It responds well to certain objects which are important to its survival, particularly flies, but surely its visual world must be far less rich than ours. Is our visual world restricted by the limitations of our eyes and brains?

There are fish which can detect weak electric fields, and locate objects which distort their self-made fields. These fish have a sense entirely foreign to us, and yet we know a great deal more about electrical fields than they do; and we have learned to develop instruments which locate objects in the same way and more efficiently. Our brain has largely overcome this limitation of our sensory apparatus. Similarly, we have learned a great deal about the stars and their composition from the most meagre sensory evidence, by making deductions and using the slender evidence to test guesses and hypotheses. Our eyes are general-purpose instruments for feeding the brain with comparatively undoctored information, while the eyes of animals possessing simpler brains are more elaborate, for they filter out information which is not essential to their survival, or usable by the simple brain. It is this freedom to make new inferences from sensory data which allows us to discover and see so much more than other animals. The

12·1 Michotte's apparatus for investigating perception of cause. The rotating disc carries lines. A small section of each line is viewed through a fixed slot. The visible sections move along the slot, depending on their shape on the disc. (Thus a co-axial circle would be stationary, while any other form will move.) Michotte finds that when one moves and touches another, which then moves off, its movement seems to be *caused* by the blow of the first.

viewing slot in mask        rotating disc

large brains of mammals, and particularly humans, allow past experience and anticipation of the future to play a large part in augmenting sensory information, so that we do not perceive the world merely from the sensory information available at any given time, but rather we use this information to test hypotheses of what lies before us. Perception becomes a matter of suggesting and testing hypotheses. We see this process of hypothesis-testing most clearly in the ambiguous figures, such as the Necker cube (figure 1·4). Here the sensory information is constant (the figure may even be stabilised on the retina) and yet the perception changes from moment to moment, as each possible hypothesis comes up for testing. Each is entertained in turn, but none is allowed to stay when no one is better than its rival hypotheses.

The continual searching for the best interpretation is good evidence for the general importance of augmenting the limitations of the senses by importing other knowledge; but the ambiguous figures show this system at a curious disadvantage because they give no clue of which bet to make, and so it never settles for a bet. The great advantage of an active system of this kind is that it can often function in the absence of reliable information, like a good officer in battle. But it must sometimes make a wrong decision. It is possible to draw figures apparently representing objects, which nevertheless cannot correspond to real objects. Several examples have been designed by L. S. and R. Penrose: two are shown in figure 12·2. They look all right at first sight, but as objects they are impossible – the eye roves around trying to discover the sense of them, but never finds a solution.

Extreme emotional stress may upset the system, much as stress can distort intellectual judgment, giving the kind of terrible but false reality expressed most dramatically by Macbeth:

> Is this a dagger which I see before me,
> The handle toward my hand? Come, let me clutch thee:
> I have thee not, and yet I see thee still.
> Art thou not, fatal vision, sensible
> To feeling as to sight? or art thou but
> A dagger of the mind, a false creation,
> Proceeding from the heat-oppressed brain?
> Mine eyes are made the fools o' the other senses,
> Or else worth all the rest: I see thee still
> And on the blade and dudgeon gouts of blood,
> Which was not so before. There's no such thing:
> It is the bloody business which informs
> Thus to mine eyes.

Why should the perceptual system be so active in seeking alternative solutions, as we see it to be in ambiguous situations? Indeed, it seems more active, and more intellectually honest in refusing to stick with one of many possible solutions, than is the cerebral cortex as a whole – if we may judge by the tenacity of irrational belief in politics or religion. The perceptual system has been of biological significance for far longer than the calculating intellect. The regions of the cerebral cortex concerned with thought are comparatively juvenile. They are self-opinionated by comparison with the ancient striate area responsible for seeing.

The perceptual system does not always agree with the rational thinking cortex. To the cortex the distance of the moon is four hundred thousand km.; to the visual part of the brain it is a mere few hundred metres. Though in this instance the cortical view is the correct one, the striate area is never informed, and we still see the moon as though it lay almost within our grasp.

The visual brain has its own logic and preferences, which are not understood cortically. Some objects are beautiful, others ugly; but we have no idea, for all the theories which have been put forward, why this should be so. The answer lies a long way back in the history of the visual part of the brain, and is lost to the new mechanisms which give our intellectual view of the world.

We think of perception as an active process of using information to suggest and test hypotheses. Clearly this involves learning, and whatever the final answer on the importance of perceptual learning in babies, it does seem clear that knowledge of non-visual characteristics affects how objects are seen. This is true even of people's faces: a friend or a lover looks quite different from other people; a smile is not just a baring of the teeth, but an invitation to share a joke. The blind man S.B. (chapter 11) never learned to interpret facial expressions; they meant nothing to him, though he could read a mood from the sound of a voice. Hunters can recognise birds in flight at incredible distance by the way they fly: they have learned to use related differences to identify objects which look the same to other people. We find the same with doctors diagnosing X-rays or microscope slides for signs of abnormality. There is no doubt that perceptual learning of this kind does take place, but in spite of all the evidence we still do not know for certain how far learning is required for the basis of perception.

It is not difficult to guess why the visual system has developed the ability to use non-visual information and to go beyond the immediate evidence of the senses. By building and testing hypotheses, action is directed not only to what is sensed but to what is likely to happen, and it is this that matters. The brain is in large part a probability computer, and our actions are based on the best bet in a given situation. The human brain makes efficient use of its rather limited sensory information – in the same kind of way astronomers discover the distance and the constitution of the stars by inference. Indeed, science may be thought of as co-operative perceiving.

If the brain were unable to fill in gaps and to bet on meagre evidence, activity as a whole would come to a halt in the absence of sensory inputs. In fact we may slow down and act with caution in the dark, or in unfamiliar surroundings, but life goes on and we are not powerless to act. Of course we are more likely to make mistakes (and to suffer hallucinations or illusions) but this is a small price to pay for gaining freedom from immediate stimuli for determining behaviour, as in the insects which are helpless in unfamiliar surroundings. A frog will starve to death surrounded by dead flies. Reflex action ceases without stimuli.

Most machines are controlled by their inputs. A car which does not respond systematically to the steering wheel, the accelerator or the brakes is dangerous. We design most machines to be predictable, so that they respond in expected ways, for then they are generally more useful and safer. But when we consider machines which do make decisions on their own account, this is no longer true. An automatic pilot has several kinds of information fed into it, and it may select a flight course according to a number of criteria. It is possible to make machines which will play chess, and they may surprise their designer. In short, if the machine is capable of dealing with problems, it is not always best to make its behaviour predictable, or precisely controlled by its inputs.

Is it possible to make a machine to see objects? Machines have been made which will respond to the letters of the alphabet, or other shapes, and this is not too difficult. More interesting, some of them can make the best bet as to which letter or shape it is if they are presented in unusual positions, or if parts are missing. It is even possible to make machines which will learn to distinguish shapes by discovering their singular features.

Seeing machines are in their infancy; they are crude and extremely expensive. It may be that the detailed study of eyes and brains may suggest more efficient ways of designing such machines, and they would be of great value. Mechanised offices and banks use character-recognition machines, but generally special characters are used to make the recognition easier and more reliable for the machine. One day it may be that a machine could perceive unusual objects and report back to us. This would be of the greatest use in industry, medicine, and exploration of alien worlds.

A difficulty in making a machine to perceive objects as we do, is that if it is to make inferences and test hypotheses it must be equipped with a lot of knowledge about the world of objects and how they behave. It is not enough to make an 'eye' and an electronic 'brain'; the 'brain' must be stored with a great deal of information so that its sensory information can be used to select from among the possibilities. This selection is all too familiar to the scientist. Making a new observation is extraordinarily difficult, but once made it seems obvious – and everybody else may then see it without difficulty. To design a machine to accept new objects and report them accurately, using its stored knowledge, would be a difficult though not an impossible task, which may well be realised as computer technology advances.

Finally, what happens to the human perceptual system in unfamiliar situations? This is a matter of consequence in science, where observations may be of unique events, and it is a matter of some concern in human space travel where men are required to make decisions when their senses receive unfamiliar inputs. This is like asking a computer to produce the right answer to a problem it has not been programmed to solve. There is no doubt that the human being does not do well when suddenly placed in an unfamiliar environment, but with experience he can learn to accept novel kinds

12·2 'Impossible figures' by L. S. and R. Penrose. We see these as more than mere patterns. We are, however, incapable of seeing them as possible objects, although (as has recently been shown) objects can be made to give these projections as retinal images: when the real objects look just as impossible as the figures. (See the author's book *The Intelligent Eye*, 1970.)

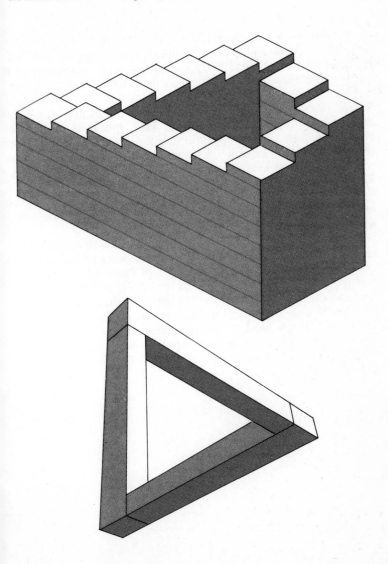

of information. We see this in trainee pilots, and in medical students using microscopes and X-ray machines. At first they are lost, but gradually they come to make appropriate decisions accurately and reliably. But there must be a limit to the reliability of perception and it can go very wrong even in familiar situations. The 'impossible figures' (figures 12·2 and 13·3) are simple line drawings which we can *see* but we cannot see correctly. They appear as impossible objects. In fact, objects appearing as the apparently impossible objects in figure 12·2 can be made. When viewed from certain positions these objects appear just as impossible as the figures. There are, then, solutions to the perceptual problem: what object is represented by this image in the eye? There can be simple objects which we cannot see. They remain impossible to see even when one has made them oneself and lived with them for years.

It seems that perception involves the interpretation of patterns in terms of objects by following rules and accepting certain assumptions. Consider the 'impossible triangle' of figure 12·2; we assume that the sides all lie in the plane of the paper, and that the edges touch at each corner. An object consisting of three edges not in a plane, with only optical coincidence at one of the 'corners', gives this figure. Recent work on programming computers to recognise objects, from television camera inputs, uses heuristic programs involving rules and assumptions – which in certain cases also lead to errors and paradoxes.

# 13 Eyes in space

Eyes and brains have evolved through geological history; they have by faltering steps come to serve their owners, by giving knowledge of certain aspects of the world important to the life and survival of their owners. The sensory systems of creatures are adapted to give, on the whole, the information which is important to the way of life of the owner – insects have remarkable perception of rapid motion; the hawk has extremely high visual acuity, allowing it to discern very small objects from a height, while the human eye is a general purpose, rather unspecialised receptor, providing the brain with a great range of information which, because of its enormous size, it is capable of handling.

If animals are removed from their normal environment they will often die because the receptor systems are too specialised. As we have said, a frog surrounded with dead flies will starve to death; a caterpillar on the leaves of an unfamiliar tree may starve. But man can live in a great variety of environments, and given products of civilisation such as houses, local control of climate, ships and aircraft, he can live in virtually any place on earth or under the sea. But as we have seen, when we use our senses in unfamiliar conditions they can mislead. The eye is less efficient when the observer is carried passively, in a car or plane, than when information of movement is available through the limbs in contact with the earth. Efficiency may be improved in some cases by experience – perceptual learning may enable the senses to work in situations never before encountered in their evolutionary development – but this is not always possible. When man is called upon to survive in extremely exotic conditions such as fast aircraft or in space vehicles, it can happen that the sensory system is basically inadequate for the tasks it is called upon to do; it is then necessary to augment the sensory system with man-made aids, generally electronic devices such as radar.

The situation of man in space is particularly interesting, visual judgment is all-important, while the available information for setting scale and distance is limited and potentially misleading. Very possibly colonies will be set up on the moon and some of the planets, but at the moment the aim of space travel is to obtain information about space conditions and to use space for making observations of distant parts of the universe, to which end a moon-based observatory would be invaluable. It is sometimes suggested that since men are so difficult to keep alive in small space vehicles, it might be better to send up packets of instruments to do the same job – to report on the nature of the universe beyond the earth. For many purposes this has proved a sound scheme, for example to get measures of radiation over long periods of time, and to discover the spectrum of the sun beyond the atmosphere. Most dramatic, however, were the pictures of the moon from automatic cameras (figures 13·1 and 13·2) and later, Mars. Direct reports of a human observer seeing the moon's surface from that distance might not have added anything much to what was learned by studying the photographs radioed back to earth. The situation is different when it comes to actively exploring the moon's surface. Although it is possible to land a tractor-like device fitted with television eyes which will crawl across the moon; if it is to explore in the full sense it must ask questions and carry out improvised experiments, and this is asking a lot from a robot. If we are to learn about the moon and planets in detail, it seems essential to send men there and rely to some extent upon their eyes and brains, though they are called upon to do tasks they were not developed to perform. We must think here of the astronaut as an elaborate sensory and decision-making device who is being asked to carry out tasks for which he was not designed, and we should try to establish how reliable he is likely to be under these conditions.

## Hazards of space

We have already seen that there are illusions which can be extremely misleading. It is time to consider just how misleading or dangerous such illusions are likely to be in space travel.

The first hazard is perceptual isolation. In experiments, largely carried out in D. O. Hebb's laboratory at McGill University, it has been found that some people experience hallucinations, as well as a general falling off in their ability to concentrate or solve problems, after hours or days of isolation. It seems that the sensory system requires a more or less continuous stream of information or it starts to go off on its own, as in extreme fatigue or under the action of certain drugs such as opium or lysergic acid. Now is there likely to be trouble of this kind? Space journeys up to the time of writing have been far from boring – and the astronauts have been kept pretty busy so that isolation has been no problem. The matter was, however, taken sufficiently seriously to be accepted as a reason for discontinuing one-man space flights, and for journeys to the moon not to be taken by one man alone. Given that the ship has a crew of several the problem should not be very different from a long ocean voyage, where there is no great difficulty in providing sufficient activity and variety to keep men from experiencing severe psychological disturbance, though of course plain old-fashioned boredom does remain a problem.

Absence of gravity in a space ship is another matter of some concern, but at this time we know nothing definite about the effects of zero gravity over long periods. There is a suspicion that there may be marked physiological effects, particularly upon the vascular system, but surprisingly little has been reported upon the effects, if any, on perception. We have seen that rotation of the visual world with prisms can be in some sense compensated, but what happens when it is not clear what is 'up' and what is 'down'? It seems that in the weightless state the observer tends to accept his own feet as 'below' and his head as 'above', but there could well be ambiguity in some circumstances, so that he could be disoriented, and there may be some odd visual effects. The practical importance of disorientation or illusions will, of course, depend upon what the astronauts are called upon to do. When leaving their ships, to float about in space, we should expect some pretty odd effects. If they assemble orbiting space stations, we can predict certain disturbing effects with some confidence. We started out by considering certain figures which are ambiguously seen in depth,

13·1 No eye had ever seen this – the back of the moon, photographed by a Russian rocket in October 1959.

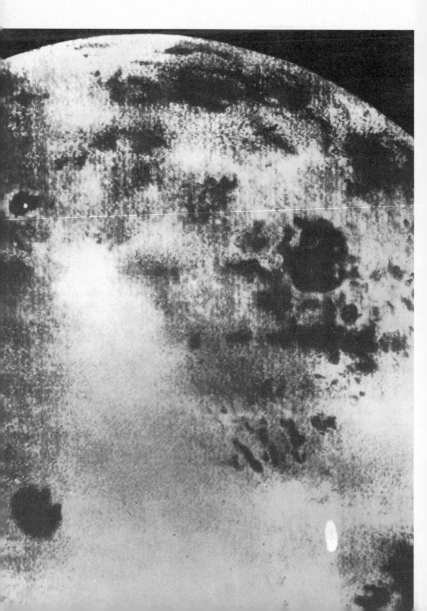

13·2 Nearer than an eye had been – a small region of the front of the moon, photographed by the American moon probe, Ranger 7, in July 1964.

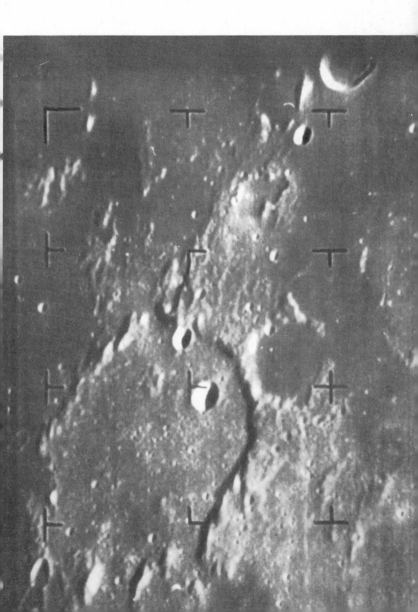

for example the Necker cube, and we went on to point out that *all* retinal images are essentially ambiguous since any image could represent any of an infinite set of objects at different orientation. Now, as we have seen, there is generally sufficient information available to determine with reasonable certainty the correct interpretation of retinal images, but this will not so often be true in space. Space is a black curtain, studded with brilliant stars. The spider-web girders and struts of a space station would appear brilliant, luminous, against the curtain of space. There would be no more cues to the distance of the parts than we get from the luminous glowing figures we use for our experiments already described when we tried to isolate the essential features of depth perception, and discover the origins of the distortion illusions (chapter 9).

Except when there was a textured background, size constancy followed apparent distance – the apparently further face of the luminous Necker cube appearing larger than the front face, whichever this might be – and we should expect the same of the parts of the orbiting space station. The struts and girders will lie ambiguously in depth. When the truly further parts are seen as nearer, the structure will look distorted. It will swing round with the observer when he moves; instead of against his movements as by normal motion parallax. This will be true when he knows he is moving, but an interesting point arises: *will* he know that he is moving (unless he is looking at artificial near objects and so has motion parallax available to him)? The answer seems to be, so far as one can determine it in an earthbound laboratory, that he will tend to regard small acceleration forces as indicating movement, and his visual perception will be affected by this assumption. If he jets himself along with an air blast, in the best science-fiction tradition, a distant object seen as near will shrink when he jets himself toward it, as we may see by experimenting with after-images in darkness. They shrink and expand as we move, provided they are regarded as staying stationary in space, and we should expect the same of actual luminous objects whose distance is seen as greater

13·3 A most curious impossible figure. The trouble comes from the ambiguity of depth – the eye is given conflicting information to locate the parts in depth, and the brain cannot make up its mind!

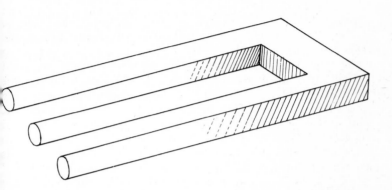

than it really is, when the image does not in fact change in the eye (figure 13·3). We have measured this effect in the author's laboratory, using electronically produced luminous displays which are made to shrink or expand with the observer's movements. By making it shrink as he approaches it, until he sees no change, we can calculate the extent of this illusion, which is due to size constancy being set by information of his movement. We find that his size constancy scaling is greater when he moves forwards than backwards, so we can expect this asymmetry in the conditions of space. It increases with increase of information of his movements away from or towards the display.

The fact that perceptual interpretation of depth can be entirely reversed is in some cases extremely serious. Consider not space travel, but its cousin – flying. When landing an aircraft it is possible that the pilot's perception of the runway may be reversed as in the luminous Necker cube. If this happened, the runway would appear to move with him rather than against him. Its size and shape would be seen wrong, and he would be most likely to make reversed correction movements of the plane's controls. What has happened is that his visual input is effectively reversed and so whatever needs correcting will be corrected exactly wrongly. If the pilot would normally pull back on the stick, to raise the nose of the plane, he will now push it down, with consequences all too easy to imagine. This perceptual reversal is most probable at night, or in fog, when there is no detailed texture to determine what is nearer and what further. It is most likely when the more distant lights are the brighter. Brightness is a clue to distance, bright lights appearing closer than dim ones when there is no other information available, and so it is possible for an unfortunate arrangement of lights to be generally seen reversed in depth. It would seem important to consider this matter in designing airport lighting. Disturbing in this connection is the surprising fact that other information does not prevent these visual reversals, though added information can reduce the chance of them occurring. When the luminous cube is held in the hand, it will still reverse though the situation is impossible, the hand experiencing one object and the eye another although they are clearly the same. When the cube is rotated in the hand the effect is extraordinary, for by touch it rotates in one direction while by vision it rotates in the opposite direction. It feels as though the wrist is dislocated, and in spite of this bizarre experience the visual system will not come to terms, but continues to give a reversed view of the world, which could be disastrous.

We may return to eyes and brains on an alien world. As an example of being misled by the unfamiliar, the writer recently visited the desert in New Mexico, staying on a mountain from which there was a view across the desert to mountains on the other side of the whole range. They appeared to be twenty to thirty kilometres away but in fact they are one hundred kilometres distant, across the desert. It would be impossible for a man to walk to them, carrying enough food and water to live. After the misty English climate, the dry air of the desert gave a totally misleading indication of the distance of the mountains. We should expect this sort of thing dramatically on the moon and planets where the atmosphere and lighting conditions are very different from earth's, and also where the scale of objects is very different. We have seen (chapter 10) that shadows are important for seeing depth, the sun serving as a 'third eye' – Heaven knows what happens to human perception on a world having two suns!

It may well be that in discovering space we will learn about ourselves. We can wear reversing spectacles but we cannot on earth avoid gravity. The effects of such alien conditions which cannot be simulated on earth are of great interest, and it is important to use the space-travel situation to learn more about perception and its limitations, not only for the benefit of the astronaut but to discover the limits of human perception.

## Seeing machines

The camera is passive, and represents only the first and simplest stage of perception; can we design and make a complete visual machine? It would be most useful for space travel, if it could survive extreme conditions, require small operating power and survive for long periods, perhaps many hundreds of years, to report to our descendants on distant regions of space. But we are far from designing a machine which will come anywhere near perceiving the world as we see it. Indeed, this has proved the most intractable problem to the cybernetic attempt to explain the brain in terms of engineering design. We think of the brain as a computer, and we believe that perceiving the world involves a series of computer programming tricks, especially heuristic rule following – which must lead to errors in sufficiently atypical situations. Computers fed with 'visual' information from television cameras and programmed to interpret their 'retinal' patterns in terms of objects are now being built. The results of ancient evolutionary experiments are just being transferred to technology, to blur the distinction between men and machines, until perhaps we (and they) may say without hesitating that machines 'see', 'think' and 'understand'. Until we can make machines like this we will not fully understand the human eye and brain.

# Bibliography

If a book has been published both in the United Kingdom and North America both publishers are listed, the British one being listed first. Dates, except where otherwise stated, are of first publication. References to journals are abbreviated in accordance with the *World List of Scientific Periodicals*.

### General books

E. G. Boring, *Sensation and Perception in the History of Experimental Psychology*, Appleton-Century-Croft, 1942; D. E. Broadbent, *Perception and Communication*, Pergamon, 1958; J. S. Bruner et al., *Contemporary Approaches to Cognition*, O.U.P./Harvard, 1957; T. N. Cornsweet, *Visual Perception*, Academic Press, 1970; J. J. Gibson, *The Perception of the Visual World*, Allen & Unwin/Houghton Mifflin, 1950; J. J. Gibson, *The Senses Considered as Perceptual Systems*, Boston, Houghton Mifflin, 1966. D. O. Hebb, *The Organization of Behaviour*, Chapman & Hall/Wiley, 1949; H. von Helmholtz, *Handbook of Physiological Optics* (1867), ed. J. P. C. S. Southall, Dover reprint, 1963; J. E. Hochburg, *Perception*, Prentice Hall, 1964; H. W. Leibowitz, *Visual Perception*, Collier/Macmillan, 1965; M. H. Pirenne, *Vision and the Eye*, Chapman & Hall/Anglobooks, 1948; M. D. Vernon, *A Further Study of Visual Perception*, C.U.P., 1952; L. Zuzne, *Visual Perception of Form*, Academic Press, 1970.

### Collected papers

D. C. Beardslee, and M. Wertheimer (eds.), *Readings in Perception*, van Nostrand, 1958; R. N. Haber (ed.), *Contemporary Theory and Research in Visual Perception*, Holt, Rinehart and Winston, Inc., 1968.

### 2 Light

See F. A. Jenkins and H. E. White, *Fundamentals of Optics*, McGraw-Hill, 3rd ed., 1957, and W. Bragg, *Universe of Light*, Bell/Clarke, Irwin, 1962.

### 3 In the beginning

There is no book describing primitive eyes in detail, but more developed eyes are described magnificently in G. L. Walls, 'The vertebrate eye and its adaptive radiation', *Cranbrook Institute of Science Bulletin* **19,** 1942.

The eyes of insects are described by V. B. Wigglesworth, in *The Principles of Insect Physiology*, Methuen/Wiley, 5th ed., 1953. Recent investigation of the eye of *Copilia* is described by R. L. Gregory, H. E. Ross, and N. Moray, in 'The curious eye of *Copilia*', *Nature, Lond.* **201,** 1166, (1964).

#### 4 The eye

For the general structure of the eye, see T. C. Ruch and J. F. Fulton *Medical Physiology and Biophysics*, Saunders, 18th ed., 1960. It is described in great detail in H. Davson (ed.), *The Eye*, Academic Press, 1962. This work is a most useful source book of physiological optics.

The problem of how the eye accommodates to different distances is particularly interesting because the image at the retina is the same whether the eye is accommodated too far or too near; there is thus no available signal for giving the sign of an error. This problem has been investigated with an ingenious technique due to Campbell and Robson: see F. W. Campbell and J. G. Robson, 'High-speed infra-red optometer', *J. opt. Soc. Amer.* **49,** 268 (1959).

The full story of the control of the size of the pupil by intensity of light is complicated. See F. W. Campbell and T. C. D. Whiteside, 'Induced pupiliary oscillations', *Brit. J. Ophthal.* **34,** 180 (1950). For a very clear full account see L. Stark, 'Servo analysis of pupil reflex', *Medical Physics*, Vol. 3, ed. O. Glasser, Year Book, Chicago, 1960.

The retina is described most generously in *The Retina* by S. L. Polyak, C.U.P./Chicago, 1941.

Eye movements were first investigated by R. Dodge, 'An experimental study of visual fixation', *Psychol. Monogr.* **8,** No. 4 (1907). Eye movement control is described in 'Central control of eye movement', by E. Whitteridge. *Handbook of Physiology – Neurophysiology*, Vol. II, chapter XLII. Optical stabilisation of retinal images is described by L. A. Riggs, E. Ratliff, J. C. and T. N. Cornsweet, 'The disappearance of steadily fixated visual test objects', *J. opt. Soc. Amer.* **43,** 495 (1953). A recent and very simple technique is described by R. M. Pritchard, 'A collimator stabilising system for the retinal image', *Quart. J. exp. Psychol.* **13,** 181 (1961). The effect of stabilising is described by R. W. Ditchburn and B. L. Ginsborg, 'Vision with a stabilised retinal image', *Nature, Lond.* **170,** 36 (1950); and R. M. Pritchard, W. Heron, and D. O. Hebb, *Canad. J. Psychol.* **14,** 67 (1960).

The most complete account of binocular vision is given by K. N. Ogle, *Researches in Binocular Vision*, Saunders, 1950. The experiments demonstrating the ability of the brain to perform cross-correlations to give depth from a pair of random but related patterns is described by Julesz: see B. Julesz, *Foundations of Cyclopean Perception*, University of Chicago Press, 1971.

## 5 The brain

The structure of the brain is described in any physiology textbook, e.g. Fulton, op. cit. A general discussion of structure and function is given by C. U. M. Smith, *The Brain: Towards an Understanding*, Faber and Faber, 1970; and a useful account covering briefly an unusual range of topics is to be found in D. E. Wooldridge, *The Machinery of the Brain*, McGraw-Hill, 1963. The history of ideas on the brain and sensation is given by K. D. Keele in *Anatomies of Pain*, Blackwell/Machwith, 1957. The recent, and now accepted, theory of action potentials in nerves is described in B. Katz, 'How cells communicate', *Sci. Amer.* **205**, 3 (1961), and more technically by F. Crescitelli, 'Production and transmission in the central nervous system', *Annu. Rev. Physiol.*, **17**, 243 (1955).

The important work on discovering the neural mechanism responding to specific angles of lines, shapes and movements for the cat's brain is due to D. H. Hubel and T. N. Wiesel, 'Receptive fields, binocular interaction and functional architecture in the cat's visual cortex', *J. Physiol.* **160**, 106 (1962), and other papers in the same journal. For related work on the retina of the frog see J. Y. Lettvin, H. R. Maturana, W. S. McCulloch, and W. H. Pitts, 'What the frog's eye tells the frog's brain', *Proc. Inst. Radio Engrs. N.Y.* **47**, 1940 (1959). Recent experiments show that the basic feature detectors are affected by, and require, specific visual stimulation: C. Blakemore and G. F. Cooper, 'Development of the brain depends on the Visual Environment', *Nature*, **228**, 477–8 (1970).

## 6 Seeing brightness

Until fairly recently the accepted theory of dark-light adaptation is that due to Selig Hecht, 'The nature of the photo receptor process', described in C. Murchison (ed.), *Handbook of General Experimental Psychology*, O.U.P./Clark U.P., 1934. Doubt was cast on the completeness of this theory by many experiments, including those of K. J. W. Craik: 'The effect of adaptation on differential brightness discrimination', *J. Physiol.* **92**, 406 (1938); and K. J. W. Craik and M. D. Vernon, 'The nature of dark adaptation', *Brit. J. Psychol.*, **32**, 62 (1941). It has recently been greatly modified by the important work of Rushton: see W. A. H. Rushton and F. Campbell, 'Measurement of rhodopsin in the living human eye', *Nature, Lond.* **174**, 1096 (1954), and many later papers.

Lateral inhibition in the retina is discussed by S. W. Kuffler, 'Discharge patterns and functional organisation of mammalian retina', *J. Neurophysiol.*

**16**, 37 (1953); and, for the frog's retina, H. B. Barlow, 'Summation and inhibition in the frog's retina', *J. Physiol.* **119**, 69 (1953). It is discussed in relation to other visual functions, by H. B. Barlow, 'Temporal and spatial summation in human vision at different background intensities', *J. Physiol.* **141**, 337 (1958).

The Pulfrich Effect was first described by Pulfrich, in *Naturwissenschaften* **10**, 569 (1922), and is discussed by G. B. Arden and R. A. Weale, 'Variations in the latent period of vision', *Proc. Roy. Soc. B.* **142**, 258 (1954).

There is an enormous literature on the absolute sensitivity of the eye. The classical paper on the quantal efficiency of the eye is S. Hecht, S. Schlaer, and M. H. Pirenne, 'Energy quanta and vision', *J. Gen. Physiol.* **25**, 819 (1942). The important method of estimating the number of quanta required for detection using frequency-of-seeing curves is described best by M. H. Pirenne, *Vision and the Eye*, (chapters 6, 7, and 8), Chapman and Hall/Anglobooks, 1948. This is an extremely useful short book.

The important work on recording from the optic nerve of *Limulus* is mainly due to Hartline: see H. K. Hartline, 'The neural mechanisms for vision', *The Harvey Lectures* **37**, 39 (1942), The nerve messages in the fibres of the visual pathway', *J. opt. Soc. Amer.* **30**, 239 (1940).

The suggestion that visual detection may be limited by neurological noise, was first made by a television engineer: see A. Rose, *Proc. Inst. Radio Engrs. N.Y.* **30**, 293 (1942). The idea has been developed by several investigators, notably by Barlow: see H. B. Barlow, 'Retinal noise and the absolute threshold', *J. opt. Soc. Amer.* **46**, 634 (1956), and 'Incremental thresholds at low intensities considered as signal noise discriminations', *J. Physiol.* **136**, 469 (1957). Psychophysical decision theory dates from W. P. Tanner and J. Swets, 'A Decision-Making Theory of Visual Detection', *Psychol. Rev.*, **61**, 401–409 (1954). The attempt to see tactually is described by P. Bach-y-Rita, C. C. Collins, B. W. White, F. Saunders, L. Scaddon and R. Blomberg, 'Vision Substitution by Tactile Image Projection', *Nature*, **221**, 963–964 (1969).

## 7 Seeing movement

For data on thresholds for detecting movement, see: J. F. Brown, *Psychol. Bull.* **58**, 89 (1961). More sophisticated measurements are given by H. W. Leibowitz, 'The relation between the rate threshold for perception of movement for various durations and exposures', *J. exp. Psychol.* **49**, 209 (1955).

The stability of the visual world during eye movements is considered by H. von Helmholtz, op. cit. For the 'outflow' theory, see E. von Holst, 'Relations between the central nervous system and the peripheral organs', *Brit. J. Anim. Beh.* **2**, 89 (1954); and R. L. Gregory, 'Eye movements and the stability of the visual world', *Nature, Lond.* **182**, 1214 (1958).

Literature on the autokinetic effect is reviewed by R. L. Gregory and O. L. Zangwill, 'The origin of the autokinetic effect', *Quart. J. exp. Psychol.* **15**, 4 (1963), where evidence for the muscle-fatigue theory is given.

The waterfall effect is described in most detail by A. Wohlmgemuth, 'On the after-effect of seen movement', *Brit. J. Psychol. Monogr.* **1** (1911). The effect occurs only when the retina is stimulated with movement; that it is limited to adaptation of the image/retina system is shown by S. M. Anstis and R. L. Gregory, 'The after-effect of seen motion: the role of retinal stimulation and eye movements', *Quart. J. exp. Psychol.*, 1964. The apparent movement known as the phi phenomenon has been discussed mainly by the Gestalt school: see in particular M. Wertheimer, *Z. Psychol.* **61**, 161 (1912), who named the phenomenon. The time-interval-distance relations of the two lights, giving apparent movement of a perceptually single light moving from one to the other (Korte's Law) were given by A. Korte in K. Koffka (ed.), *Beiträge zur Psychologie der Gestalt*, Kegan Paul, 1919. The effect is in fact extremely variable. A good account is to be found in M. D. Vernon, op. cit.

The cognitive effect of induced movement was first investigated by K. Duncker, 'Induced motion', in W. H. Ellis (ed.), *Source Book of Gestalt Psychology*, Routledge/Harcourt Brace, 1938.

## 8 Seeing colour

There is no single clear treatment of colour vision, but a useful collection of classical papers is to be found in R. C. Teevan and R. C. Birney (ed.), *Colour Vision*, Van Nostrand, 1961. This contains Thomas Young's classical paper, 'On the theory of light and colours', as well as those of Helmholtz. E. H. Land, 'Experiment in Colour Vision', *Sci. Amer.* **5**, 84 (1959), is also included. See also M. H. Wilson and R. W. Brocklebank, 'Two-colour projection phenomena', *J. phot. Sci.* **8**, 141 (1960), and D. B. Judd, 'Appraisal of Land's work on two-primary colour projections', *J. opt. Soc. Amer.* **50**, 254 (1960).

For experiments on the effect of adaptation on colour matches, see G. S. Brindley, *Physiology of the Retina and the Visual Pathway*, Arnold/ Waverley Press, 1960.

## 9 Illusions

For a good discussion on dreaming, see I. Oswald, *Sleeping and Waking, Physiology and Psychology*, Elsevier, Amsterdam, 1962, and I. Oswald, 'The experimental study of sleep', *Brit. med. Bull.* **20,** 70 (1964). Effects of drugs are discussed by A. Summerfield, 'Drugs and human behaviour', *Brit. med. Bull.* **20,** 70 (1964), and H. Steinberg, 'Drugs and animal behaviour', *Brit. med. Bull.* **20,** 75 (1964). These papers are excellent reviews and contain extensive bibliographies.

The work of Wilder Penfield on eliciting memories and other experiences by direct stimulation of the brain is described in W. Penfield and L. Roberts, *Speech and Brain Mechanisms*, O.U.P., 1959. The effect of repeated patterns giving visual disturbance has been investigated by D. M. McKay, who has found some dramatic effects. These are discussed in his paper, 'Interactive processes in visual perception', in *Sensory Communication*, ed. W. A. Rosenblith, M.I.T. Press and Wiley, 1961.

The first important experimental work on estimating size and shape constancy (following the realisation of the problem by Descartes) was undertaken by Robert Thouless. See R. H. Thouless, 'Phenomenal regression to the real object 1', *Brit. J. Psychol.* **21,** 339 (1931); and 'Individual differences in phenomenal regression', *Brit. J. Psychol.* **22,** 216 (1932). Thouless used a technique involving comparisons between two objects, generally discs of cardboard, placed at different orientations or distances. A different technique, which can be used for measuring constancy during movement, is described by S. M. Anstis, C. D. Shopland, and R. L. Gregory, 'Measuring visual constancy for stationary or moving objects', *Nature, Lond.* **191,** 416 (1961). Some results of this technique are described in R. L. Gregory and H. E. Ross, 'Visual constancy during movement', *Perceptual & Motor Skills.* **18,** 3 and 23 (1964). A general discussion of visual distortion, giving the historical theories with references, is to be found in R. S. Woodworth, *Experimental Psychology*, Methuen/ Holt, 1938. One of the first hints of the kind of theory advocated in this book is to be found in R. Tausch, *Psychologische Forschung* **24,** 299 (1954). The first statement of the theory advocated here is R. L. Gregory, 'Distortion of visual space as inappropriate constancy scaling', *Nature, Lond.* **119,** 678 (1963). Evidence of visual scaling applying to touch is given by J. P.

Frisby and I. R. L. Davies, 'Is the haptic Muller-Lyer a Visual Phenomenon?' *Nature*, **231**, 5303 (1970). An investigation of the puzzling problem of similar distortions for touch is due to R. G. Rudel and H-L Teuber, 'Decrement of visual and haptic Muller–Lyer illusion on repeated trails: a study of crossmodal transfer', *Quart. J. exp. Psychol.* **15**, 125 (1963). The occurrence (or rather, lack) of illusions in primitive people is discussed, with the evidence, by M. H. Segall, T. D. Campbell, and M. J. Herskovitz. *The Influence of Culture on Visual Perception*, Bobbs Merril, N.Y. (1966).

## 10 Art and reality

Ames' demonstrations are best described in W. H. Ittleson, *The Ames Demonstrations in Perception*, O.U.P./Princeton, 1952. Gibson's important work, only briefly touched on here because he has described it so well himself, is to be found in J. J. Gibson, *The Perception of the Visual World*, Allen & Unwin/Houghton-Mifflin, 1950. The best attempt at relating the problems of the artist to what we know of visual perception is E. H. Gombrich, *Art and Illusion*, Phaidon/Pantheon, 1960.

## 11 Do we have to learn how to see?

A discussion of cases of recovery from blindness up to 1932 is to be found in M. von Senden, *Space and Sight*, tr. P. Heath, Methuen/Free Press, 1960. These cases came into prominence in the psychological literature with D. O. Hebb's important book, *The Organisation of Behaviour*, Chapman & Hall/Wiley, 1949. The most recent case is described by R. L. Gregory and J. G. Wallace, 'Recovery from early blindness: a case study', *Exp. Psychol. Soc. Monogr. No. 2*, Cambridge, 1963. This contains the full account of the case of S. B. described briefly in the chapter.

For the work of recording eye movements of young babies see R. L. Fantz, 'The Origin of Form Perception', *Sci. Amer.* **204,** 66 (1961).

For experiments on animals reared in darkness, see E. H. Hess, 'Space perception in the chick', *Sci. Amer.* **195**, 71 (1956); A. H. Reisen, 'The development of perception in man and chimpanzee', *Science* **106**, 107 (1947); A. H. Reisen, 'Arrested vision', *Sci. Amer.* **183**, 16 (1950).

For Stratton's work, see 'Some preliminary experiments on vision', *Psychol. Rev.* **3**, 611 (1896); 'Vision without inversion of the retinal image', *Psychol. Rev.* **4**, 341 (1897), and *Psychol. Rev.* **4**, 463 (1897). The rather more sophisticated work of Ewert is described by him in 'A study of the effect of inverted retinal stimulation upon spatially co-ordinated behaviour', *Genet. Psychol.*

*Monogr.* 7, 177 (1930); and two papers on 'Factors in space localization during inverted vision', *Psychol. Rev.* **43**, 522 (1936), and **44**, 105 (1937). This was followed up in J. & J. K. Peterson 'Does practice with inverting lenses make vision normal?', *Psychol. Monogr.* **50**, 12 (1938). Further references, and original work especially on displacement of images in time will be found in K. U. and W. M. Smith, *Perception and Motion: an Analysis of Space-structured Behavior*, Saunders, 1962. The important work of Richard Held and his colleagues on adaptation in humans to displacing prisms is given in many papers: see R. Held and A. Hein, 'Movement-produced stimulation in the development of visually guided behavior', *J. Comp. and Phys. Psychol.* **56**, 872 (1963), for the experiment described in the text.

The first paper on the effect of distorting spectacles is J. J. Gibson, 'Adaptation, after-effect and contrast in the perception of curved lines', *J. exp. Psychol.* **16**, 1 (1933). Figural after-effects are described in W. Köhler and H. Wallach, 'Figural after-effects', *Proc. Amer. phil. Soc.* **88**, 269 (1944), and C. E. Osgood and A. W. Heyer, 'A new interpretation of figural after-effects', *Psychol. Rev.* **59**, 98 (1951). For a review on orientation see I. P. Howard and W. B. Templeton, *Human Spatial Orientation*, Wiley (1966). Evidence of very early object recognition is given by T. G. R. Bower, 'The Object in the World of the Infant', *Scient. Amer.*, **225**, 4 (1971).

## 12 Seeing and believing

Michotte's work on seeing causality is described by him in *The Perception of Causality*, T. R. and E. Miles, ed., Methuen, 1963.

The 'impossible figures' are due to L. S. Penrose and R. Penrose, 'Impossible objects: a special type of illusion', *Brit. J. Psychol.* **49,** 31 (1958). For papers, see in L. Uhr (ed.), *Pattern Recognition*, Wiley (1966). For a development of themes in this book see R. L. Gregory, *The Intelligent Eye*, Weidenfeld and Nicolson (1970).

# Acknowledgments

I would like to thank particularly Dr Stuart Anstis and my other colleagues and students who have discussed the problems of this book with me, pointed out errors, and helped with experiments. I have benefited by the personal generosity of many people in the United States, especially: Professors J. J. Gibson, H-L. Teuber, Warren McCulloch and F. Nowell Jones. The book was largely written during a visit to Professor Jones's department at U.C.L.A.

It is not possible to give due credit to all the authors of the papers and books one has read over ten or more years, but I certainly owe particular debts to Drs M. H. Pirenne, J. J. Gibson, E. H. Gombrich, and many more. The various illegible manuscripts were typed with unfailing cheerfulness and intelligence by my secretary, Mrs Olive Faircloth, without whom life would be impossible. Mrs Monica Beck kindly helped me with the index.

My interest in the subject started with the teaching of Professor Sir Frederic Bartlett, FRS, and was encouraged and guided by Professor O. L. Zangwill.

I would like to thank Mrs Audrey Besterman and Miss Mary Waldron for drawing the diagrams and the Illustration Research Service, London, for collecting the colour plates used.

Acknowledgment is due to the following for illustrations: 1·2 C. E. Osgood and Oxford University Press; 2·1 10·2 The British Museum; 2·2, 8·1 The Royal Society; 2·4 The Bodleian Library; 3·1 G. L. Walls and *Cranbrook Institute of Science Bulletin*; 3·2 M. Rudwick; 3·3 V. B. Wigglesworth, Methuen & Co., Ltd and John Wiley & Sons, Inc.; 3·3, 3·5 R. L. Gregory, H. E. Ross, N. Moray and *Nature*; 4·2 T. C. Ruch, J. F. Fulton and W. B. Saunders Co.; 4·5 Medical Illustrations Department, Institute of Ophthalmology, London; 4·8 R. M. Pritchard and *Quarterly Journal of Experimental Psychology*; 4·16 Bela Julesz and *Science* (Vol. 145, 24 July 1964, pp. 356–62), © 1964 by the American Association for the Advancement of Science; 5·2 W. Penfield, T. Rasmussen and The Macmillan Co., New York; 5·4. The British Broadcasting Corporation; 5·6, 5·7 D. H. Hubel, T. H. Wiesel and the *Journal of Physiology*; 6·6, 6·7, 6·8 H. K. Hartline and Academic Press, Inc., 7·1, 9·1. The Mansell Collection; 7·4 R. L. Gregory, O. L. Zangwill and *Quarterly Journal of Experimental Psychology*; 8·3 W. D. Wright and Henry Kimpton; 8·4 S. Hecht Murchisson and Clark University Press; 9·9 Rania Massourides; 9·12, 10·16 Derrick Witty; 9·17 J. Allen Cash; 10·1 Drawings Collection, Royal Institute of

248

British Architects; 10·3 Bibliothèque de l'Institut de France; 10·4 John Freeman; 10·5 by courtesy of the Trustees of the National Gallery, London; 10·8, 10·9, 10·10 *Punch*; 10·11 Eastern Daily Press, Norwich; 10·13 J. J. Gibson, Allen & Unwin, Ltd and Houghton Mifflin Company; 11·1 William Vandivert and *Scientific American*; 11·2, 11·3 R. L. Gregory, J. G. Wallace and *Experimental Psychology Society*; 11·4 R. L. Fantz and *Scientific American*, photo David Linton; 11·9 I. Kohler and *Scientific American*; 11·11, 11·12, 11·13 K. U. and W. M. Smith and W. B. Saunders Co.; 12·1 A. Michotte, Methuen & Co. Ltd and Basic Books, Inc., Publishers; 12·2 L. S. and R. Penrose and *British Journal of Psychology*; 13·1, 13·2 London and Wide World Photos; 13·3 Ed Morrett and Whifin Machine Co.

R.L.G.

# Index

# World University Library

Other titles in this international series

## Economics and Social Studies

**The World Cities**
Peter Hall, *Reading*

**The Economics of Underdeveloped Countries**
Jagdish Bhagwati,
*M.I.T.*

**Development Planning**
Jan Tinbergen,
*Rotterdam*

**Leadership in New Nations**
T. B. Bottomore,
*Vancouver*

**Human Communication**
J. L. Aranguren,
*Madrid*

**Education in the Modern World**
John Vaizey, *Oxford*

**Soviet Economics**
Michael Kaser, *Oxford*

**Decisive Forces in World Economics**
J. L. Sampedro, *Madrid*

**Power and Society in Africa**
Jacques Maquet,
*California*

**Key Issues in Criminology**
Roger Hood and
Richard Sparks,
*Cambridge*

**Population and History**
E. A. Wrigley,
*Cambridge*

## History

**The Old Stone Age**
François Bordes,
*Bordeaux*

**The Emergence of Greek Democracy**
W. G. Forrest, *Oxford*

**Rome: The Story of an Empire**
J. P. V. D. Balsdon,
*Oxford*

**Muhammad and the Conquests of Islam**
Francesco Gabrieli,
*Rome*

**The Civilisation of Charlemagne**
Jacques Boussard,
*Poitiers*

**The Italian City-Republics**
D. P. Waley, *London*

**Humanism in the Renaissance**
S. Dresden, *Leyden*

**The Rise of Toleration**
Henry Kamen, *Warwick*

**The Scientific Revolution 1500-1700**
Hugh Kearney,
*Edinburgh*

**The Dutch Republic**
C. H. Wilson,
*Cambridge*

**The Left in Europe**
David Caute, *Oxford*

**The Rise of the Working Class**
Jürgen Kuczynski,
*Berlin*

**Chinese Communism**
Robert North, *Stanford*

## Language and Literature

**Western Languages AD 100-1500**
Philippe Wolff,
*Toulouse*

**Two Centuries of French Literature**
Raymond Picard, *Paris*

**Russian Writers and Society 1825-1904**
Ronald Hingley, *Oxford*

**Satire**
Matthew Hodgart,
*Sussex*

## The Arts

**Twentieth Century Music**
H. H. Stuckenschmidt,
*Berlin*

## Art Nouveau
S. Tschudi Madsen,
*Oslo*

## Palaeolithic Cave Art
P. J. Ucko and
A. Rosenfeld, *London*

## Expressionism
John Willett, *London*

## Philosophy and Religion

### Christian Monasticism
David Knowles,
*London*

### The Papacy and the Modern World
K. O. von Aretin,
*Göttingen*

### Witchcraft
Lucy Mair, *London*

### Religious Sects
Bryan Wilson, *Oxford*

## Applied Science

### Words and Waves
A. H. W. Beck,
*Cambridge*

### The Science of Decision-making
A. Kaufmann, *Paris*

### Bionics
Lucien Gerardin, *Paris*

### Biomedical Engineering
H. S. Wolff, *London*

### Data Study
J. L. Jolley, *London*

## Physical Science and Mathematics

### The Quest for Absolute Zero
K. Mendelssohn, *Oxford*

### Particles and Accelerators
Robert Gouiran,
*C.E.R.N., Geneva*

### What is Light?
A. C. S. van Heel and
C. H. F. Velzel,
*Eindhoven*

### Mathematics Observed
Hans Freudenthal,
*Utrecht*

### Quanta
J. L. Andrade e Silva
and G. Lochak, *Paris*.
Introduction by
Louis de Broglie

## Psychology and Human Biology

### The Molecules of Life
Gisela Nass, *Munich*

### The Biology of Work
O. G. Edholm, *London*

### The Psychology of Fear and Stress
J. A. Gray, *Oxford*

### The Tasks of Childhood
Philippe Muller,
*Neuchâtel*

### The Doctor and the Patient
P. Lain Entralgo,
*Madrid*

### Chinese Medicine
P. Huard and M. Wong,
*Paris*

## Zoology and Botany

### Mimicry in Plants and Animals
Wolfgang Wickler,
*Seewiesen*

### Lower Animals
Martin Wells,
*Cambridge*

**The World of an Insect**
Rémy Chauvin, *Strasbourg*

**Life in the Sea**
Gunnar Thorson, *Elsinore*

**Plant Variation and Evolution**
S. M. Walters and D. Briggs, *Cambridge*

**Plant Cells**
R. Buvat, *Paris*

**The Age of the Dinosaurs**
Björn Kurtén, *Helsinki*

## Earth Sciences and Astronomy

**The Structure of the Universe**
E. L. Schatzman, *Paris*

**Climate and Weather**
H. Flohn, *Bonn*

**Anatomy of the Earth**
André Cailleux, *Paris*

**Sun, Earth and Radio**
J. A. Ratcliffe, *Cambridge*